THE CALIFORNIA DIRECTORY OF
FINE WINERIES

THIRD EDITION

The California Directory of
Fine Wineries

Marty Olmstead, Writer

Robert Holmes, Photographer

Tom Silberkleit, Editor and Publisher

Wine House Press

CONTENTS

INTRODUCTION

Whether you are a visitor or a native seeking the ultimate chalice of nectar from the grape, navigating Northern California's wine country can be intimidating. Hundreds of wineries—from glamorous estates to converted barns, from nationally recognized labels to hidden gems—are found throughout Napa, Sonoma, and Mendocino. The challenge is deciding where to go and how to plan a trip. This book will be your indispensable traveling companion.

The sixty wineries in this fully updated, third edition of *The California Directory of Fine Wineries* are known for producing some of the world's most admired wines. From the moment you walk in the door of these wineries, you will be greeted like a guest and invited to sample at a relaxing, leisurely tempo. Although the quality of the winemaker's art is of paramount importance, the wineries are also notable as tourist destinations. Many boast award-winning contemporary architecture, while others are housed in lovingly preserved historical structures. Some have galleries featuring museum-quality artwork by local and international artists or exhibits focusing on the region's past and the history of winemaking. You will also enjoy taking informative behind-the-scenes tours, exploring inspirational gardens, and participating in celebrated culinary programs.

As you explore this magnificent region, you'll encounter some of California's most appealing scenery and attractions—mountain ranges, rugged coastline, pastures with majestic oak trees, abundant parkland, renowned spas, and historic towns. Use the information in this book to plan your trip, and be sure to stop along the way and take in the sights. You have my promise that traveling to your destination will be as pleasurable as the wine tasted upon your welcome.

—Tom Silberkleit
Editor and Publisher
Wine House Press
Sonoma, California

THE ETIQUETTE OF WINE TASTING

Most of the wineries profiled in this book offer amenities ranging from lush gardens to art exhibitions, but their main attraction is the tasting room. This is where winery employees get a chance to share their products and knowledge with consumers, in hopes of establishing a lifelong relationship. They are there to please.

Yet, for some visitors, the ritual of tasting fine wines can be intimidating. Perhaps it's because swirling wine and using a spit bucket seem to be unnatural acts. But with a few tips, even a first-time taster can enjoy the experience. After all, the point of tasting is to enhance your knowledge by learning the differences among varieties of wines, styles

of winemaking, and appellations. A list of available wines is usually posted, beginning with whites and ending with the heaviest reds or, if available, dessert wines. Look for the tasting notes, which are typically set out on the counter; refer to them as you taste each wine.

After you are served, hold the stem of the glass with your thumb and as many fingers as you need to maintain control. Lift the glass up to the light and note the color and intensity of the wine. Good wines tend to be bright, with the color fading near the rim. Next, gently swirl the wine in the glass. Observe how much of the wine adheres to the sides of the glass. If lines—called legs—are visible, the wine is viscous, indicating body or weight as well as a high alcohol content. Now, tip the glass to about a 45-degree angle, take a short sniff, and concentrate on the aromas. Swirl the wine again to aerate it, releasing additional aromas. Take another sniff and see if the "bouquet" reminds you of anything—rose petals, citrus fruit, or a freshly ironed pillowcase, for example—that will help you identify the aroma.

Finally, take a sip and swirl the wine around your tongue, letting your taste buds pick up all the flavors. The wine may remind you of honey or cherries or mint—as with the "nosing," try to make as many associations as you can. Then spit the wine into the bucket on the counter. Afterward, notice how long the flavor stays in your mouth; a long finish is the ideal. If you don't want another taste, just pour the wine remaining in your glass into the bucket and move on. Remember, the more you spit or pour out, the more wines you can sample. Many tasting rooms offer flavorless crackers for refreshing your palate between wines.

The next level of wine tasting involves guided tastings and food-and-wine pairings. Often a few cheeses or a series of appetizers will be paired with a flight of wines, usually a selection of three red or three white wines presented in the correct order of tasting. The server will explain what goes with what.

If you still feel self-conscious, practice at home by swirling water in a glass, taking a sniff and a sip, then spitting it out into a container. Once in a real tasting room, you'll be better able to focus on the wine itself. That's the real payoff, because once you learn what you like and why you like it, you'll be able to recognize wines in a similar vein anywhere in the world.

WHAT IS AN APPELLATION?

The word *appellation* is often used to refer to the geographical area where wine grapes were grown. If the appellation is named on the bottle label, it means that at least 85 percent of the wine is from that area.

The terms "appellation of origin" and "American Viticultural Area" (AVA) are frequently used interchangeably in casual conversation, but they are not synonymous. In the United States, appellations follow geopolitical borders, such as state and county lines, rather than geographic boundaries. AVAs are defined by such natural features as soil types, climate, and topography.

Since 1978, the U.S. Bureau of Alcohol, Tobacco and Firearms (BATF) has been the arbiter of what does and does not qualify as an AVA. A winery or other interested party that wants a particular area to qualify as an official AVA must supply proof to the BATF that it has enough specific attributes to distinguish it significantly from its neighbors.

Why do winemakers care? Because it is far more prestigious—and informative—to label a wine with an appellation such as Sonoma County, Napa Valley, or Russian River Valley than with the more generic California, which means the grapes could have come from the Central Valley or anywhere else in the state. Moreover, informed consumers learn that a Chardonnay from the Alexander Valley, for instance, is apt to taste different from one originating in the Russian River Valley.

A winery may be located in one appellation but use grapes from another to make a particular wine. In this case, the appellation on the label would indicate the source of the grapes rather than the physical location of the winery. For example, Ledson Winery and Vineyards is in the Sonoma Valley but makes a Pinot Noir using grapes from the Russian River Valley. Thus the bottle is labeled "Ledson Winery and Vineyards Pinot Noir, Russian River Valley."

The following are the appellations in Napa, Sonoma, and Mendocino:

NAPA	SONOMA	MENDOCINO
Atlas Peak	Alexander Valley	Anderson Valley
Chiles Valley District	Bennett Valley	Cole Ranch
Diamond Mountain District	Chalk Hill	Dos Rios
Howell Mountain	Dry Creek Valley	McDowell Valley
Los Carneros	Green Valley	Mendocino
Mount Veeder	Knight's Valley	Mendocino Ridge
Napa Valley	Los Carneros	North Coast
North Coast	North Coast	Potter Valley
Oak Knoll District	Northern Sonoma	Redwood Valley
Oakville	Rockpile	Sanel Valley
Rutherford	Russian River Valley	(proposed viticultural area)
Spring Mountain District	Sonoma Coast	Ukiah Valley
St. Helena	Sonoma Mountain	(proposed viticultural area)
Stags Leap District	Sonoma Valley	Yorkville Highlands
Wild Horse Valley		
Yountville		

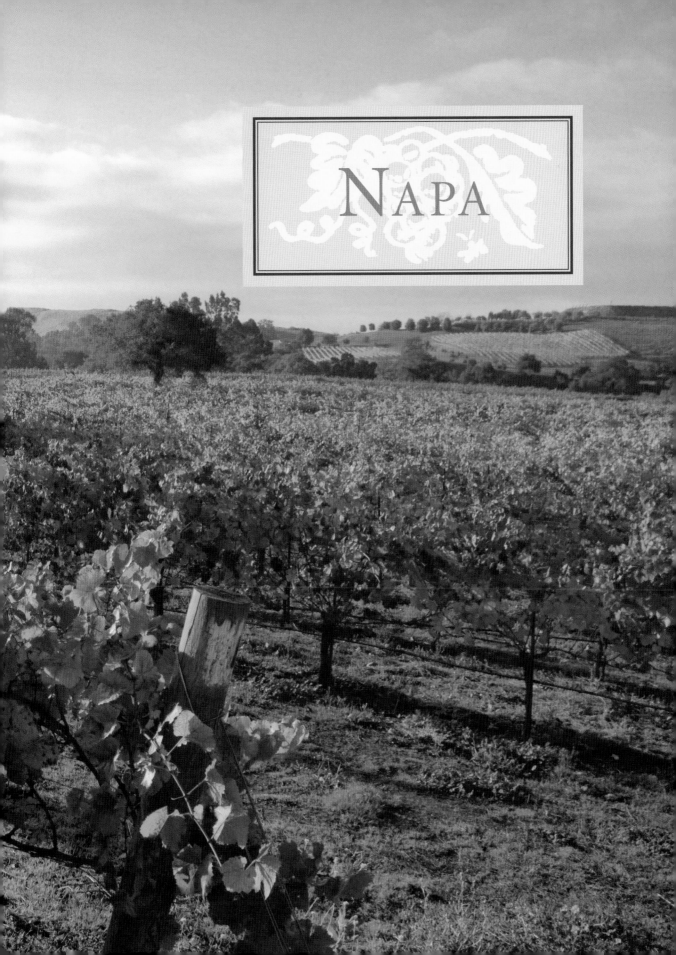

NAPA

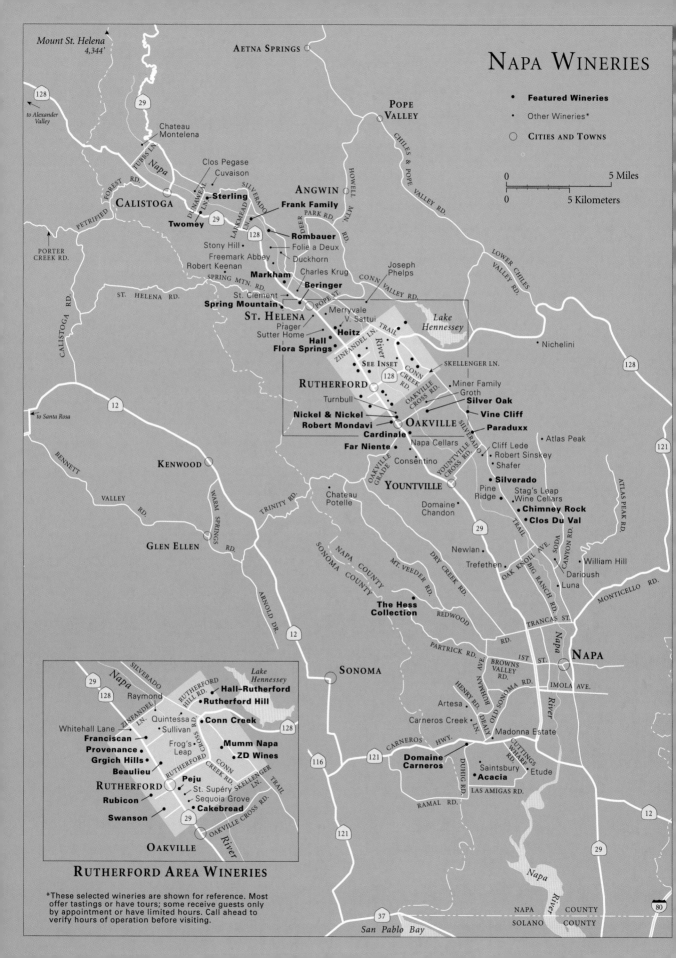

NAPA WINERIES

- ● **Featured Wineries**
- · Other Wineries*
- ○ CITIES AND TOWNS

0 _____ 5 Miles
0 _____ 5 Kilometers

Mount St. Helena 4,344'

AETNA SPRINGS

POPE VALLEY

128
to Alexander Valley

29

Chateau Montelena

Clos Pegase
Cuvaison

ANGWIN

Sterling
Frank Family

CALISTOGA

Twomey

29
128

Rombauer

Stony Hill
Freemark Abbey
Robert Keenan

Folie a Deux
Duckhorn

Markham
Charles Krug
Beringer

Joseph Phelps

PORTER CREEK RD.

ST. HELENA RD.

SPRING MTN. RD.

St. Clement
Spring Mountain

ST. HELENA

Merryvale
V. Sattui

Lake Hennessey

LOWER CHILES VALLEY RD.

CALISTOGA RD.

Prager
Sutter Home
Heitz
Hall
Flora Springs

SEE INSET

· Nichelini

128

RUTHERFORD

128

SKELLENGER LN.

to Santa Rosa

12

Turnbull

Miner Family
Groth
Silver Oak

KENWOOD

Nickel & Nickel
Robert Mondavi

OAKVILLE

Vine Cliff
Paraduxx

Napa Cellars

121

VALLEY RD.

Cardinale
Far Niente

Consentino

Cliff Lede
· Atlas Peak
Robert Sinskey
Shafer

WARM SPRINGS RD.

GLEN ELLEN

Chateau Potelle

YOUNTVILLE

Silverado
Pine Ridge
Stag's Leap
Wine Cellars
Chimney Rock
Clos Du Val

TRINITY RD.

Domaine Chandon

29

Newlan
Trefethen

· William Hill
Darioush
Luna

ATLAS PEAK RD.

BENNETT

SONOMA COUNTY

NAPA COUNTY

MT. VEEDER RD.

DRY CREEK RD.

OAK KNOLL AVE.

SODA CANYON RD.

MONTICELLO RD.

12

The Hess Collection

REDWOOD

TRANCAS ST.

NAPA

SONOMA

PARTRICK RD.

BROWNS VALLEY RD.

IMOLA AVE.

BUHMAN AVE.

HENRY RD.

DEALY LN.

OLD SONOMA RD.

1ST. ST.

116

Artesa
Carneros Creek

Madonna Estate

CUTTINGS WHARF RD.

121

CARNEROS HWY.

Domaine Carneros

Saintsbury
Acacia

Etude

DUHIG RD.

121

LAS AMIGAS RD.

RAMAL RD.

29

80

RUTHERFORD AREA WINERIES

29
128

Napa

SILVERADO

Raymond

RUTHERFORD HILL RD.

Lake Hennessey

Hall-Rutherford
Rutherford Hill

Whitehall Lane
Quintessa
Sullivan

Conn Creek

128

Franciscan
Provenance
Grgich Hills
Beaulieu

Frog's Leap

Mumm Napa
ZD Wines

RUTHERFORD

Peju
St. Supéry
Sequoia Grove

Rubicon

Cakebread

Swanson

29

OAKVILLE

River

*These selected wineries are shown for reference. Most offer tastings or have tours; some receive guests only by appointment or have limited hours. Call ahead to verify hours of operation before visiting.

37

San Pablo Bay

NAPA COUNTY
SOLANO COUNTY

Napa River

The most famous winemaking region in the United States, the Napa Valley is a microcosm of the California Wine Country, with hundreds of wineries and thousands of acres of vineyards amassed in a narrow valley less than thirty miles long. This patchwork of agriculture extends north from the upper San Pablo Bay to the dramatic palisades that tower over Calistoga. On the east, it is defined by a series of hills known as the Vaca Range. On  the opposite border, the western horizon is dominated by the rugged peaks of the Mayacamas Range, including the steep, forested slopes of Mount Veeder.

The best way to get an overview is to take a hot-air balloon ride that departs at daybreak for a cool, calm flight above the vineyards and usually concludes with a champagne breakfast. The second-best way is to drive up the Oakville Grade and pull over at the top for a post-card-perfect view.

The county's largest cities are Napa and St. Helena, where you will find many shops and major attractions. Charming small towns along Highway 29, the main thoroughfare that is mostly only two lanes wide, have restaurants, inns, spas, and other businesses that cater to visitors.

ACACIA VINEYARD

Mother Nature makes her presence known at this hidden spot in southernmost Napa County more than almost anywhere else in wine country. The vineyards of the Carneros extend from the rolling hills all the way to the marshes of San Pablo Bay, where twenty-five species of waterfowl join the resident eagles and owls that swoop above the grapevines and acacia groves. Yellow mustard blankets the lime green vineyards in winter until buds break and grapes begin to emerge beneath their trellised canopies. Warm weather eventually turns the grape leaves a deeper green, followed by yellow and orange in the heat of autumn.

This vista surrounds the winery at Acacia Vineyards, which was named for the once-plentiful trees that flutter with bright yellow flowers in early spring. Founded in 1979, the winery was one of the first in the state to establish a reputa- tion for vineyard-designated Pinot Noir. In 1996 Acacia began acquiring the land sur- rounding the winery, eventu- ally assembling a 150-acre estate vineyard. Today, the majority of Acacia's fruit is estate grown; the remainder comes from other leading Carneros sources, including Sangiacomo Vineyard, Beckstoffer Vineyard, and St. Clair Vineyard. Acacia's most recent acquisition is Winery Lake, a vineyard long prized for its Pinot Noir and Chardonnay grapes.

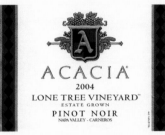

Pinot Noir and Chardonnay are the two grape varieties most associated with the Carneros region, a swath of land in southern Sonoma and Napa. The marine influence of San Pablo Bay mod- erates summertime heat, extending the growing season for these slow-maturing grapes. Vineyards were planted here in the late nineteenth century, but the Carneros did not shine as a winemaking region until the late 1970s. The founders of Acacia were among the first winemakers in contemporary history to realize the area's potential for producing fine wines.

Due to the growing popularity of Acacia's wines, a decade after the winery's founding, the building was enlarged and remodeled. Double glass doors lead into the compact tasting room, where appointments are necessary to guarantee elbow space, especially on busy weekends. On one wall is a stunning aerial photograph of the winery, its vineyards, and the marshes of San Pablo Bay in the distance. Much the same view is available from almost every spot on the estate, and visitors can borrow binoculars for a better look. To help ensure the viability of the Carneros as a wildlife habitat, the winery contributes to the state's wetland restoration efforts through sales of Acacia Marsh Chardonnay, which is available only in the tasting room.

ACACIA VINEYARD
2750 Las Amigas Rd.
Napa, CA 94559
707-226-9991
877-226-1700
acacia.info@acaciavineyard.com
www.acaciavineyard.com

OWNER: Diageo Chateau and Estate Wines.

LOCATION: Less than 5 miles south of the town of Napa.

APPELLATION: Los Carneros.

HOURS: 10 A.M.–4 P.M. Monday–Saturday, 12–4 P.M. Sunday.

TASTINGS: By appointment. $10 tasting fee.

TOURS: Weekdays, by appointment.

THE WINES: Chardonnay, Pinot Noir, Viognier.

SPECIALTIES: Single-vineyard Chardonnay and Pinot Noir.

WINEMAKER: Anthony King.

ANNUAL PRODUCTION: 100,000 cases.

OF SPECIAL NOTE: Single-vineyard series Pinot Noir and Chardonnay and Acacia Marsh Chardonnay available only in tasting room. Acacia also makes a sparkling wine in limited amounts.

NEARBY ATTRACTIONS: COPIA: The American Center for Wine, Food and the Arts (winemak- ing displays, art exhibits); Napa Valley Opera House (live performances in historic building); di Rosa Preserve (indoor and outdoor exhibits of works by contemporary Bay Area artists).

BEAULIEU VINEYARD

BEAULIEU VINEYARD
1960 St. Helena Hwy.
Rutherford, CA 94573
800-264-6918, ext. 5233
visitingbv@bvwines.com
www.bvwines.com

OWNER: Diageo Chateau &
Estate Wines.

LOCATION: About 3 miles
south of St. Helena.

APPELLATIONS: Rutherford
and Napa Valley.

HOURS: 10 A.M.–5 P.M. daily.

TASTINGS: $10 for
Appellation Tasting
(5 wines); $25 for Reserve
Tasting (5 wines).

TOURS: Call for
information.

THE WINES: Cabernet
Sauvignon, Chardonnay,
Merlot, Pinot Gris, Pinot
Noir, Port, Sangiovese,
Sauvignon Blanc, Shiraz,
Syrah, Viognier, Zinfandel.

SPECIALTIES: Cabernet
Sauvignon, Chardonnay,
Pinot Noir.

WINEMAKERS: Joel Aiken,
Jeffrey Stambor, and
Domenica Totty.

ANNUAL PRODUCTION:
1.5 million cases.

OF SPECIAL NOTE: Annual
events include Georges
de Latour Private Reserve
Cabernet Sauvignon
Release Party (September
or October), Older Vintage
Tasting Event (December).
Library wines available for
tasting and purchase.

NEARBY ATTRACTIONS:
Bothe-Napa State Park
(hiking, picnicking, horseback riding, swimming
Memorial Day–Labor
Day); Culinary Institute
of America at Greystone
(cooking demonstrations).

Well into its second century as a leading Napa Valley winery, Beaulieu Vineyard has yet to rest on its laurels. In 2005 the winery completely remodeled its Reserve Room to provide an appropriately rarefied setting for some of the most widely collected Napa Valley Cabernet Sauvignons. Subdued lighting, stone walls, goldstone pavers, and Douglas fir ceiling beams create an almost reverential ambience. The rectangular mahogany tasting bar is topped with off-white Carrera marble, a perfect background for examining the viscosity and color of wines. According to Michael Guthrie of MG&Co Architects in San Francisco, the Reserve Room was "designed to convey a respect for the past with a vision toward the future."

The winery expresses respect for its heritage in other ways. Just outside the entrance is a bronze statue of legendary Beaulieu wine-maker André Tchelistcheff. While founder Georges de Latour's name is on the label of Beaulieu's most famous wines, the man known as "the Maestro" is credited with their creation.

De Latour was born in south-western France to landed gentry whose vineyards were destroyed by the phylloxera root louse. He immi-grated to the United States in 1896, settling in the Sonoma County town of Healdsburg. When he visited nearby Napa Valley, he was struck by the area's similarities to the Medoc. He and his wife, Fernande, determined to establish their own winery, managed to buy four acres in Rutherford, which they named Beaulieu ("beautiful place"). To keep his vineyards free of the phylloxera that had infested countless California grapevines, de Latour imported French vines and grafted them onto resistant American rootstock. Thanks to his visionary entrepreneurship, Beaulieu Vineyard flourished. After Prohibition forced many wineries to close their doors, de Latour stayed in business by providing altar wine to the Catholic Church. In 1923 he bought the old stone winery across the road and began expanding its production. When repeal came in 1933, Beaulieu Vineyard was ready with a stockpile of aging, varietally labeled Cabernet Sauvignon.

It was the small but promising vintage of 1936 that prompted de Latour to find a winemaker worthy of those grapes: the brilliant, Russian-born Tchelistcheff, who came to the winery in 1938 from the Institut National Agronomique in Paris. As master enologist for thirty-five years, he helped attract international acclaim for Beaulieu Vineyard wines by the time its founder died in 1940. The Maestro came out of retirement for a few years in 1991 and worked side by side with winemaker Joel Aiken to create some of the wines now stored in the Reserve Room's library. Beaulieu Vineyard's other wines are poured in the main tasting room nearby.

BERINGER VINEYARDS

With the 1883 Rhine House, hand-carved aging tunnels, and a heritage dating to 1876, Beringer Vineyards is steeped in history like few other wineries in California. The oldest continuously operating winery in the Napa Valley, it combines age-old traditions with up-to-date technology to create a wide range of award-winning wines.

It was German know-how that set the Beringer brothers on the path to glory. Jacob and Frederick Beringer emigrated from Mainz, Germany, to the United States in the 1860s. Jacob, having worked in cellars in Germany,  was intrigued when he heard that the California climate was ideal for growing the varietal grapes that flourished in Europe's winemaking regions. Leaving Frederick in New York, he traveled west in 1870 to discover that the Napa Valley's rocky, well-drained soils were similar to those in his native Rhine Valley. Five years later, he bought land with Frederick and began excavating the hillsides to create tunnels for aging his wines. The brothers founded Beringer Vineyards in 1876. During the building of the caves and winery, Jacob lived in an 1848 farmhouse now known as the Hudson House. The meticulously restored and expanded structure now serves as Beringer Vineyards' Culinary Arts Center.

But the star attraction on the lavishly landscaped grounds is unquestionably the seventeen-room Rhine House, which Frederick modeled after his ancestral home in Germany. The redwood, brick, and stucco mansion is painted in the original Tudor color scheme of earth tones, and the original slate still covers the gabled roof and exterior. The interior is graced with myriad gems of craftsmanship such as Belgian art nouveau–style stained-glass windows.

The winery's standard tour encompasses a visit to the cellars and the hand-dug aging tunnels in the Old Stone Winery, where tasting is available. Beringer also offers programs that provide visitors more in-depth experiences. The Vintage Legacy Tour focuses on the winery's history. The Historic District Tour emphasizes points of historic interest such as the Rhine House and aging caves. The Taste of Beringer Tour includes a visit to the original St. Helena Home Vineyard and proceeds through the Old Stone Winery prior to a special wine tasting in the historic Rhine House.

BERINGER VINEYARDS
2000 Main St.
St. Helena, CA 94574
707-963-4812
www.beringer.com

OWNER: Foster's Wine Estates Americas.

LOCATION: On Hwy. 29 about .5 mile north of St. Helena.

APPELLATION: Napa Valley.

HOURS: 10 A.M.–5 P.M. daily in winter; until 6 P.M. in summer.

TASTINGS: 2 wines with tour fee; $5 for 3 nonreserve wines in Old Stone Winery; $5–16 for reserve wine flights.

TOURS: 30-minute tours ($10) on the hour, 10 A.M.– 4 P.M. Vintage Legacy Tour ($35), Historic District Tour ($20), and Taste of Beringer ($15) by reservation.

THE WINES: Cabernet Franc, Cabernet Sauvignon, Cabernet Sauvignon Port, Chardonnay, Johannisberg Riesling, Merlot, Pinot Noir, Sangiovese, Sauvignon Blanc, Syrah, White Merlot, White Zinfandel.

SPECIALTIES: Private Reserve Cabernet Sauvignon, single-vineyard Cabernet Sauvignon, Private Reserve Chardonnay.

WINEMAKERS:
Ed Sbragia, wine master; Laurie Hook, winemaker.

ANNUAL PRODUCTION: Unavailable.

OF SPECIAL NOTE: Tour includes visit to barrel storage caves hand-chiseled by Chinese laborers in late 1800s.

NEARBY ATTRACTIONS: Bothe-Napa State Park (hiking, picnicking, horse-back riding, swimming Memorial Day–Labor Day); Bale Grist Mill State Historic Park (water-powered mill circa 1846); Silverado Museum (Robert Louis Stevenson memorabilia).

CAKEBREAD CELLARS

CAKEBREAD CELLARS
8300 St. Helena Hwy.
Rutherford, CA 94573
707-963-5222
cellars@cakebread.com
www.cakebread.com

OWNERS: Cakebread family.

LOCATION: 5 miles south of
St. Helena.

APPELLATION: Napa Valley.

HOURS: 10 A.M.–4:30 P.M.
daily.

TASTINGS: By appointment;
$10 for 4 wines.

TOURS: 10:30 A.M. daily, by
reservation.

THE WINES: Cabernet
Sauvignon, Chardonnay,
Merlot, Pinot Noir,
Sauvignon Blanc, Syrah,
Zinfandel.

SPECIALTIES: Benchland
Select Cabernet
Sauvignon, Cabernet
Sauvignon, Chardonnay,
Rubaiyat (Pinot Noir/
Syrah blend), Sauvignon
Blanc.

WINEMAKER: Julianne Laks.

ANNUAL PRODUCTION:
95,000 cases.

OF SPECIAL NOTE: Cooking
classes offered sporadi-
cally throughout the year.
American Harvest Work-
shop is a 4-day food and
wine seminar held every
September for profession-
als; some lectures are open
to the public. Pinot Noir
and Syrah available only
at winery.

NEARBY ATTRACTIONS:
Napa Valley Museum
(winemaking displays,
art exhibits); Silverado
Museum (Robert Louis
Stevenson memorabilia);
balloon rides.

The winery that Jack and Dolores Cakebread founded in 1973 has always been a family endeavor. While Jack and their sons Steve, Bruce, and Dennis planted the vineyards, Dolores began the flower and vegetable gardens that would become an integral part of the winery's extensive hospitality program.

Cakebread Cellars has grown from modest beginnings—22 acres and a first vintage totaling 157 cases of 1973 Chardonnay, all of which was sold to Groezinger's Wine Shop in nearby Yountville—to a winery owning 800 acres with 425 of them planted in grapevines. Although it has become one of the Napa's best-known wineries, still has a homey feel. Dolores's bloom along the driveway and is easy to imagine the place as it ago, when the Cakebreads first

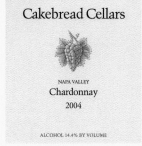

the cluster of barnlike buildings colorful plants are always in beside the small parking lot. It looked more than thirty years started their enterprise.

Today, all tours and tast- which allows the winery to host quality of visitors' experience. ings are by prior appointment, small groups and maintain the Tours, varying by the season, can include the gardens, the winemaking facility, and the vineyards. Along the way, visitors can learn about some of Cakebread's innovative techniques. For example, the vineyards that are flat are harvested at night, when the air is cool and the grapes are higher in acid and lower in sugar than when the sun comes up. And Cakebread presses its white grapes in whole clusters, which results in the fresh, fruit-forward flavors for which its Sauvignon Blanc and Chardonnay are known.

Visitors sample wines at mobile tasting stations stocked not only with the current releases but also with tasting cards containing notes on each varietal. On the back of each card is a pairing recipe that is changed for every vintage. Depending on the weather, tour guides can easily move the stations to any spot in the winery or even outdoors, where an inner courtyard is embellished with topiary and formal plantings. Valley oaks, weeping willows, manicured lawns, and a contained waterfall create a quiet oasis. On warm days, market umbrellas shade the tasting tables.

Cakebread Cellars is still a family operation. Dolores, now a master gardener, grows fresh vegetables, herbs, and edible flowers that are prized by the winery chefs, who use them in preparing appetizers for the weekly food-and-wine pairings. Bruce Cakebread is the chief operating officer, while Dennis Cakebread is in charge of sales and marketing. Jack Cakebread remains at the helm but still finds time to indulge in another passion. His photographs of friends, growers, and family members are displayed throughout the winery.

CARDINALE ESTATE

ituated in the renowned Oakville District, Cardinale Estate winery is perched atop a knoll that commands a panoramic view of the Napa Valley. On the southwest side of the winery, a balcony affords visitors the unique opportunity to view the lay of the land and locate the world-famous appellations along the valley floor, as well as along the Mayacamas and Vaca ranges. For those who want to study a particular location in detail, a telescope is available.

Surrounding the winery are low fieldstone walls built more than a century ago. Below to the

east are fields and vineyards and an there since the late nineteenth cen- thoroughly twenty-first-century op- Bordeaux blend that influential critic profound wines being produced in

Cardinale's contemporary Italian On the east side of the building, four climbing roses, support a pergola granite. On the west side, a little covered with vines curling above Mediterranean theme continues inside

CARDINALE
2003
NAPA VALLEY
CABERNET SAUVIGNON

old farmhouse that has been standing tury. Inside the winery, however, is a eration producing an ultra-premium Robert Parker deemed "one of the northern California."

architecture befits its lofty location. square stone pillars, entwined with above a flooring of decomposed courtyard is closed in by a stone wall pink coral bells and other plants. The the tasting room, with its travertine

marble floor and stone-topped bar. The design of the interior is understated: cream-colored walls, maple furnishings, and a simple ivory chandelier. The minimalist decor balances the experience of sampling the wine or appreciating the spectacular scenery visible from the tasting room. Visitors can also enjoy the wine outside, at glass-topped tables on a marble-floored deck, where they have views of Mount Veeder and one of Cardinale's mountain estate vineyards.

The profundity that Robert Parker wrote about derives from the mountain terrain of the core vineyards. Cardinale wine is primarily crafted from fruit grown on two rugged mountain estate vineyards—Keyes Vineyard on Howell Mountain and Veeder Peak Vineyard on Mount Veeder. The steep slopes have thin, rocky soils that force the vines to struggle, resulting in small berries that produce more concentrated flavors and colors than grapes grown on the valley floor with its richer soils. The rocks in the mountain soils also provide excellent drainage as well as trace elements that contribute to the complexity of the wines. Moreover, because of inversion—cold air settles on the valley floor while warm air rises—the higher elevations enjoy a longer growing season. Cardinale's special mountain vineyards have contributed to the wine's distinctive fusion of power and elegance since the 1995 vintage.

CARDINALE ESTATE
7600 Hwy. 29
Oakville, CA 94562
707-948-2643
info@cardinale.com
www.cardinale.com

OWNERS: Jackson family.

LOCATION: East side of Hwy. 29 just north of Yountville.

APPELLATION: Oakville.

HOURS: 10:30 A.M.–5 P.M. daily.

TASTINGS: $10 and $20 for counter tastings; $30 and $50 for sit-down tastings by appointment.

TOURS: None.

THE WINE: Cardinale (Bordeaux blend).

SPECIALTY: Cardinale (Bordeaux blend).

WINEMAKER: Chris Carpenter.

ANNUAL PRODUCTION: 700–900 cases.

OF SPECIAL NOTE: Atalon (Napa Valley Cabernet Sauvignon and Merlot) wines are also available for tasting.

NEARBY ATTRACTIONS: Napa Valley Museum (winemaking displays, art exhibits).

CHIMNEY ROCK WINERY

CHIMNEY ROCK WINERY
5350 Silverado Trail
Napa, CA 94558
707-257-2641
www.chimneyrock.com

OWNER: Terlato Wine
Group.

LOCATION: 3 miles south
of Yountville.

APPELLATION: Stags Leap
District.

HOURS: 10 A.M.–5 P.M. daily.

TASTINGS: $10 for 5 wines;
$20 for all-red tasting.

TOURS: Group tours by
appointment.

THE WINES: Cabernet Franc,
Cabernet Sauvignon,
Elevage (red Meritage),
Elevage Blanc, Fumé
Blanc, Rosé of
Cabernet Franc.

SPECIALTY: Cabernet
Sauvignon.

WINEMAKERS:
Elizabeth Vianna;
Douglas Fletcher, director
of winemaking.

ANNUAL PRODUCTION:
18,000 cases.

OF SPECIAL NOTE: Some
limited-production
wines available only in
tasting room.

NEARBY ATTRACTIONS: Napa
Valley Opera House (live
performances in historic
building); Napa Valley
Museum (winemaking
displays, art exhibits).

Shaded by a grove of poplar trees, Chimney Rock's pristine white Cape Dutch buildings, with their steep, slate-gray roofs and curving, arched gables, complement their pastoral setting. The distinctive architecture was inspired by the many years that the winery's founders spent in South Africa. The late Sheldon "Hack" Wilson and his wife, Stella, had worked abroad for decades in the soft drink, brewing, restaurant, and luxury hotel businesses, developing a taste for fine wine along the way. Not surprisingly, they began their search for winery property in France. When a couple of potential sites in Bordeaux failed to materialize, they turned their attention to California and found what they were looking for in the Napa Valley.

Wilson's research convinced him that the soils and micro- climates of the Stags Leap District would produce the quality of grapes for the style of wine he had in mind. When he saw the rustic Chimney Rock Golf Course, he could easily envision rows of grapevines in place of fairways. In 1980, the Wilsons purchased the golf course as well as the adjacent mountain, bulldozed nine of the eighteen holes, and planted vineyards on seventy-five acres. The first vintage was produced in 1984, and the winery's production building was completed five years later.

Douglas Fletcher was already an old hand at Stags Leap winemaking when he came on board in 1987, having worked at nearby Steltzner Vineyards. He was joined by Elizabeth Vianna, a Brazilian-born enologist who had worked at Chimney Rock as an intern in 1999 and has been winemaker since 2005. Together, they focus on handcrafting wines mostly from Bordeaux varietals. In 2000, with a new partnership with the Terlato family—who represent three generations in the wine business—the remaining fairways at Chimney Rock were converted to sixty-three acres of Cabernet Sauvignon vineyards. All of the winery's red-wine vineyards are in the Stags Leap District. The colorful name stems from the legend of an agile buck seen bounding along a jagged outcropping of rock to elude hunters. The appellation extends south along the Silverado Trail from the Yountville Cross Road for three miles, bordered on the east by craggy hillsides and on the west by the Napa River.

Picturesque at any time of year, Chimney Rock Winery is especially appealing in spring and summer, when aromatic mauve Angel Face roses climb the columns in front of the hospitality center. The tasting room has white walls and dark exposed beams. On the far side, doors open onto a courtyard set with tables, chairs, and white market umbrellas and planted with a bevy of rosebushes bearing ivory flowers.

Chimney Rock®
Cabernet Sauvignon
Stags Leap District
Napa Valley
2005
PRODUCED & BOTTLED BY CHIMNEY ROCK WINERY
NAPA, CALIFORNIA • ALCOHOL 14.1% BY VOLUME

CLOS DU VAL

That this winery has a French name is not an affectation. Owner and cofounder John Goelet's mother was a direct descendant of Françoise Guestier, a native of Bordeaux who worked for the Marquis de Segur, owner of Chateau Lafite and Latour. Clos Du Val translates as "small vineyard estate of a small valley," a modest nomenclature for a winery of its stature.

When Goelet, who is also the son of an American entrepreneur, set out on a global search for premium vineyard land, he found the ideal partner in Bernard Portet. Born in Cognac and raised in Bordeaux, Portet is a descendant of six generations of winemakers. He followed his passion with formal studies at the French winemaking schools of Toulouse and Montpelier before Goelet hired him in 1970 to establish Clos Du Val.

Portet spent two years getting a taste of the Napa Valley microclimates. At the time, the terrain of the Stags Leap District searching five continents before climate—or, technically, its cool evenings and dramatic were relatively undiscovered by winemakers. Goelet proved his faith in Portet by promptly acquiring 150 acres of land in the district. The first vintage of the new venture was a 1972 Cabernet Sauvignon, one of only five California Cabernets selected for the now-legendary "Paris Tasting" in 1976, an event that put the world on notice that the Napa Valley was a winemaking force to watch. Ten years later, the same vintage took first place in a rematch, further enhancing Clos Du Val's reputation for creating wines that stand the test of time.

In 1973, Clos Du Val purchased 180 acres in another little-recognized appellation—Carneros in southern Napa. Thirteen years later, the winery released its first Carneros Chardonnay, and four years later, its first Carneros Pinot Noir.

A driveway lined with cypress trees leads to the imposing, vine-covered stone winery, behind which the dramatic rock outcroppings of Stags Leap rise in sharp relief. In front of the tasting room are Mediterranean-style gardens, a raised lawn area with tables and chairs defined by a hedge of boxwood, and a demonstration vineyard with twenty rows of Merlot grapevines, accompanied by brief explanations of vineyard management techniques. Inside the winery, halogen lights on the high ceiling beam down on the wooden tasting bar, the unglazed earth-toned tile floor, and a corner display of merchandise bearing the winery's distinctive, curlicued logo. Glass doors on the far side look into a large fermentation room filled with oak and steel tanks. Visitors are welcome to prolong their visit by playing *pétanque* or enjoying a picnic in the olive grove.

CLOS DU VAL
5330 Silverado Trail
Napa, CA 94558
707-261-5200
800-993-9463
cdv@closduval.com
www.closduval.com

OWNER: John Goelet.

LOCATION: 5 miles north of the town of Napa.

APPELLATION: Napa Valley.

HOURS: 10 A.M.–5 P.M. daily.

TASTINGS: $5 for 4 wines (applicable to wine purchase); $20 for reserve wines.

TOURS: By appointment.

THE WINES: Cabernet Sauvignon, Chardonnay, Merlot, Pinot Noir.

SPECIALTY: Cabernet Sauvignon.

WINEMAKER: John Clews.

ANNUAL PRODUCTION: 65,000 cases.

OF SPECIAL NOTE: *Pétanque* court and picnic area in olive grove. Reserve wines available only in the tasting room.

NEARBY ATTRACTIONS: COPIA: The American Center for Wine, Food and the Arts; Napa Valley Museum (winemaking displays, art exhibits); Napa Valley Opera House (live performances in historic building).

CONN CREEK WINERY

CONN CREEK WINERY
8711 Silverado Trail
St. Helena, CA 94574
707-963-9100
info@conncreek.com
www.conncreek.com

OWNER: Ste. Michelle
Wine Estates.

LOCATION: Intersection
of Silverado Trail and
Rutherford Cross Rd.

APPELLATION: Napa Valley.

HOURS: 11 A.M.–4 P.M.
Sunday–Friday; 10 A.M.–
4 P.M. Saturday.

TASTINGS: $5 for 4 wines.

TOURS: By appointment,
11 A.M.–3 P.M.

THE WINES: Anthology (red
Bordeaux-style blend),
Cabernet Franc, Cabernet
Sauvignon, Sauvignon
Blanc.

SPECIALTIES: Bordeaux
varietals, especially
Cabernet Sauvignon.

WINEMAKER: Jeff McBride.

ANNUAL PRODUCTION:
18,000 cases.

OF SPECIAL NOTE: Barrel
sampling and blending
seminars by appointment.
Conn Creek Cabernet
Franc and Sauvignon
Blanc available only at
tasting room, which
also pours Villa Mt.
Eden Grand Reserve
Chardonnay, Pinot Noir,
and vineyard-designated
Zinfandels.

NEARBY ATTRACTIONS:
Bothe-Napa State Park
(hiking, picnicking,
horseback riding,
swimming Memorial
Day–Labor Day); Culinary
Institute of America at
Greystone (cooking
demonstrations); Silverado
Museum (Robert Louis
Stevenson memorabilia).

Conn Creek is one of the easiest-to-find wineries in the Napa Valley. Located near a well-traveled Rutherford intersection, it is housed in a simple Spanish Mediterranean-style stucco building that blends in well with the surroundings. In front, a grove of olive trees and colorful perennials thrive year-round in the California sun.

The winery was founded by William Collins, a former submarine officer, and his wife, Kathy, who named it for a seasonal tributary of the Napa River that flows through their vineyards. They planted grapes in 1967 and, six years later, established the winery and produced their first vintage. Conn Creek quickly won recognition for its red wines, particularly the 1974 Eisele Vineyard Cabernet Sauvignon. Most of the grapes for the award-winning wines produced in the early years came from the Collins Vineyard, which is so rocky that the owners had to use dynamite to break up the soil before planting. Situated alongside Highway 29 in St. Helena, Collins Vineyard has fifty-four acres of Cabernet Sauvignon, Cabernet Franc, and Merlot. Although Collins sold his winery in 1986, he maintains an exclusive long-term grape contract with Conn Creek.

The new owners, Ste. Michelle Wine Estates, decided to devote their energies to producing world-class Cabernet-based red wines, paring Chardonnay and Zinfandel from the winery's product line to do so. The legendary André Tchelistcheff, the former winemaker at Beaulieu Vineyard and a longtime consultant to Ste. Michelle, participated in the winery's transition to limited-production Bordeaux varietals. By 1990, the winery had been retooled for its new focus, with an expanded barrel room, improved storage, and the acquisition of new French oak barrels. These changes were followed a year later with the release of Anthology, the winery's Bordeaux-style blend. More changes came in 2003, when the St. Helena winery was refurbished with enhancements to the winemaking facility, retail shop, and barrel blending room. It also had a new winemaker, Jeff McBride, who had been winemaker at both Kenwood Vineyards and Dry Creek Vineyard in Sonoma County.

Conn Creek continues to pursue the goal of remaining a limited-production facility specializing in Napa Valley Cabernet Sauvignon. To meet the demand for its wines, the winery currently sources grapes from twelve of the Napa Valley's subappellations, including its own estate vineyard; Collins Vineyard; Palisades Ranch in the north valley; Stagecoach Vineyard in Napa's rugged eastern hills, a prized growing area for Cabernet Franc and Merlot; and the Carneros in the cool southern part of Napa Valley.

DOMAINE CARNEROS

An architectural tribute to its French heritage, the chateau that houses Domaine Carneros would look at home in Champagne, France. It dominates a hillside in the renowned Carneros region in southern Napa, prime growing area for the grape varieties that go into the best sparkling wine and sumptuous Pinot Noir. The opulent winery is approached by a long series of steps that climb to a grand entranceway. French marble floors, high ceilings, and decorative features such as a Louis XV fireplace mantel imbue the interior with a palatial ambience. Guests are welcome to order wines in the elegant salon, warmed by a fireplace on cool days, or on the terrace.

Established in 1987, Domaine Carneros is a joint venture between Champagne Taittinger of France and Kobrand Corpo-ration. President Director-General Claude Taittinger led the extensive search for the ideal site for making world-class sparkling wine. The Carneros region's long, moderately cool growing season and the fog that miti-gates the summer heat allow for slow, even ripening and perfect acidic balance in the Pinot Noir and Chardonnay grapes. Domaine Carneros farms four vineyards totaling 325 hundred acres in the appellation.

Harvest at Domaine Carneros begins in mid-August, when workers head out to pick grapes before dawn. A delicate balance of sugar and acidity is required for the best sparkling wine. The fruit is immediately brought to the press for the gentle extracting of the juice. From that moment through vinification, each lot is maintained separately before the exact blend is determined. The sparkling wines are made in accordance with the traditional *méthode champenoise,* in which secondary fermentation takes place in the bottle, not the tank. The grapes for Pinot Noir are gathered a week or two after the sparkling wine harvest is complete, then are fermented for ten days. After this, the juices are siphoned off, and the fruit is gently pressed to extract the remaining juice. The resulting wine is aged in French oak barrels for up to ten months before bottling.

In charge of these elaborate procedures is president Eileen Crane, who worked at Domaine Chandon and later served as winemaker and vice president of Gloria Ferrer Champagne Caves in nearby Sonoma. This experience—combined with the vision she shares with Taittinger on how to produce the elegant and delicate, yet intense sparkling wines—made her the ideal choice for over-seeing the planning and development of Domaine Carneros. Crane focuses on making the most of the winery's fortuitous combination of climate, California technology, and French expertise to create wines of great character.

DOMAINE CARNEROS
1240 Duhig Rd.
Napa, CA 94559
800-716-BRUT (2788)
www.domainecarneros.
com

OWNERS: Champagne Taittinger and Kobrand Corporation.

LOCATION: Intersection of Hwys. 121/12 and Duhig Rd., 4 miles southwest of the town of Napa.

APPELLATION: Los Carneros.

HOURS: 10 A.M.–6 P.M. daily.

TASTINGS: $6–$10 per glass, depending on variety; $14 for sampler of 3 sparkling wines or $13 for 3 Pinot Noirs.

TOURS: Complimentary public tours, 11 A.M., 1 P.M., and 3 P.M. daily. Group tours for 10 or more by appointment. Private reserved tours.

THE WINES: Brut Rosé, Le Rêve, Pinot Noir, Vintage Brut.

SPECIALTIES: *Méthode champenoise* sparkling wine, Pinot Noir.

WINEMAKER: Eileen Crane.

ANNUAL PRODUCTION: 45,000 cases.

OF SPECIAL NOTE: Table service available in salon or on terrace with panoramic views of Carneros region. Cheese plates and caviar available for purchase. Wine and French-related items sold in winery shop.

NEARBY ATTRACTIONS: di Rosa Preserve (indoor and outdoor exhibits of works by contemporary Bay Area artists); Napa Valley Opera House (live performances in historic building).

FAR NIENTE

FAR NIENTE
1350 Acacia Dr.
Oakville, CA 94562
707-944-2861
info@farniente.com
www.farniente.com

OWNER: Private partnership.

LOCATION: .9 mile west
of Hwy. 29 off Oakville
Grade.

APPELLATION: Oakville.

HOURS: 10 A.M.–4 P.M. daily.

TASTINGS: By appointment.
$50 for 5 wines, including
current releases and library
wines.

TOURS: By appointment.

THE WINES: Cabernet
Sauvignon, Chardonnay,
late-harvest Semillon/
Sauvignon Blanc.

SPECIALTIES: Napa Valley
Chardonnay, Napa
Valley (Oakville)
Cabernet Sauvignon.

WINEMAKER:
Stephanie Putnam.

ANNUAL PRODUCTION:
30,000 cases.

OF SPECIAL NOTE: Some
library wines available only
at winery. Tasting includes
a proprietary wine, Dolce,
a late-harvest white blend.

NEARBY ATTRACTIONS:
Napa Valley Museum
(winemaking displays,
art exhibits).

Hidden away on a private road just up from the Napa Valley floor, Far Niente is secluded among thirteen acres of southern-style landscaping distinguished by a great variety of texture, foliage, and blossoms. Some one hundred Autumn Gold gingko trees border the entrance drive to the winery. Farther along, towering redwoods, acacias, dogwoods, and century-old cork oak trees form a living canopy. The Far Niente gardens are famed for their collection of more than eight thousand southern azaleas, the largest single planting of the variety in California. Throughout the property, quaint touches like shaded pathways, hand-fitted flagstone stairs, and stone bridges arching across ponds create a memorable setting.

Far Niente was founded in 1885 by John Benson, a San Franciscan whose wealth was made in real estate and silver mines. To design the winery, Benson hired Hamden McIntyre, the architect for other stone wineries of the time, including Greystone, which became the Christian Brothers winery and is now occupied by the Culinary Institute of America. Benson decided to name his estate Far Niente, taken from the Italian phrase *dolce far niente*, "sweet to do nothing."

The winery prospered until 1919, when it was abandoned at the onset of Prohibition. It would remain untouched for the next sixty years, until a different kind of visionary arrived in the valley. Gil Nickel, a former guided-missile analyst with an agricultural background gleaned through his family's nursery business in Oklahoma, bought Far Niente in 1979 and crushed its first Chardonnay that same year. Three years later, the exquisitely restored winery produced its first Cabernet Sauvignon. Today, the winery continues to focus on these two varietals. Nickel was rewarded for his preservation efforts: the property is listed on the National Register of Historic Places.

After twenty-five years of being open only to the wine trade, Far Niente now offers tours and tastings to the public, by appointment. Visitors are welcomed in the winery's Great Hall, with its original stone walls, hardwood floors, and copious antiques. The tour departs from the Great Hall and includes the winery, a portion of Far Niente's forty thousand square feet of caves, the land-scaped grounds, and a collection of rare and classic cars, before returning for the tasting. Guests are served the current-release Chardonnay, Cabernet Sauvignon, and Dolce (the dessert wine made by the sister winery of the same name), plus two library selections, allowing them to get a taste of history in a bottle.

FLORA SPRINGS WINERY AND VINEYARDS

This winery's history is a cautionary tale of sorts: Be careful what you wish for. In 1977, Jerry and Flora Komes were looking for a place to relax and watch the grapes grow. Their search led them to the Napa Valley, which has countless porches with vineyard views. Even then, they weren't thinking of growing the grapes themselves, let alone making wine.

Then the couple saw the 1956 Louis M. Martini house in the western foothills. Louis had died three years previously, and the property was looking rather shabby. Two of the buildings, the 1888 Rennie Winery and the 1885 Charles Brockhoff Winery, were filled with bats, rats, and rattlesnakes. The place looked more like a ghost town than a potential residence, but it had the key ingredient: the very views that Jerry and Flora 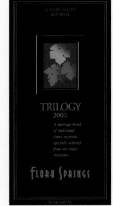 Komes desired. As Jerry recalled, "Outside of a home, it had all the things we weren't looking for."

The couple bought the pack- age and, inspired by the legacy of the land, decided to restore the property. Like so many other retirement projects, this one became a consuming passion that threatened the prospect of leisurely afternoons rocking on the porch. Before long, the property served as a magnet, luring two of Jerry and Flora's children. Son John, a general contractor and home winemaker, was fascinated by the challenges of producing wine and breathing life into the aged buildings. Daughter Julie and her husband, Pat Garvey, gave up careers in education, and Pat dedicated himself to learning the grape-growing business. Another son, Mike, also become a partner. After two vintages, John decided that he and Julie had pressed their luck as winemakers to the limit, and Ken Deis was hired. More than two decades later, he is still at it.

John's wife, Carrie, gets the credit for naming the new winery. There were two obvious life-giving sources to this venture, Flora herself and the continuously flowing springs that were the sole source of water for the property. Flora Springs had almost immediate success. The first commercially released wine, a Chardonnay, won a gold medal at the prestigious Los Angeles County Fair, the beginning of many awards for the winery.

Over the years, the family has acquired 650 acres of vineyards in nine distinct Napa Valley locations, in addition to the original Komes Ranch. The winery sells 80 percent of these grapes to twenty-five premium wineries, which gives Flora Springs a unique opportunity to select the 20 percent that fits the winery's criteria. Visitors may sample the Flora Springs wines daily at the tasting room or make an appointment to tour the winery.

FLORA SPRINGS WINERY AND VINEYARDS
Winery:
1978 W. Zinfandel Ln.
St. Helena, CA 94574
707-963-5711
info@florasprings.com
www.florasprings.com
Tasting Room:
677 St. Helena Hwy. South
St. Helena, CA 94574
707-967-8032

OWNERS: Komes/Garvey families.

LOCATION: About 1 mile south of downtown St. Helena.

APPELLATION: Napa Valley.

HOURS: 10 A.M.–5 P.M. daily (tasting room).

TASTINGS: Grand Tasting, $5 for 4 wines; Premium Tasting, $12 for 4 wines.

TOURS: Of winery by appointment.

THE WINES: Cabernet Sauvignon, single-vineyard Cabernet Sauvignons, Chardonnay, Merlot, Pinot Grigio, Sangiovese, Soliloquy (Sauvignon Blanc), Trilogy (Meritage blend).

SPECIALTY: Trilogy.

WINEMAKER: Ken Deis.

ANNUAL PRODUCTION: 45,000 cases.

OF SPECIAL NOTE: Picnic tables available at tasting room.

NEARBY ATTRACTIONS: Bothe-Napa State Park (hiking, picnicking, horse-back riding, swimming Memorial Day-Labor Day); Bale Grist Mill State Historic Park (water-powered mill circa 1846); Culinary Institute of America at Greystone (cooking demonstrations); Silverado Museum (Robert Louis Stevenson memorabilia).

FRANCISCAN

FRANCISCAN
1178 Galleron Rd.
Rutherford, CA 94574
707-967-3830
800-529-9463 (WINE)
visitorcenter@franciscan.
com
www.franciscan.com

LOCATION: Less than
3 miles south of
St. Helena.

APPELLATION: Napa Valley.

HOURS: 10 A.M.–5 P.M. daily.

TASTINGS: $5 for 4 wines;
$10 for 4 reserve wines;
$30 for private tasting by
appointment.

TOURS: Vineyard tours ($5)
by appointment.

THE WINES: Cabernet
Sauvignon, Chardonnay,
Merlot.

SPECIALTIES: Magnificat
(red Meritage), Cuvée
Sauvage Chardonnay.

WINEMAKER: Janet Myers.

ANNUAL PRODUCTION:
Unavailable.

OF SPECIAL NOTE: Certain
other wines available only
in tasting room.

NEARBY ATTRACTIONS:
Bothe-Napa State Park
(hiking, picnicking, horse-
back riding, swimming
Memorial Day–Labor
Day); Bale Grist Mill State
Historic Park (water-
powered mill circa 1846);
Silverado Museum
(Robert Louis Stevenson
memorabilia).

O ne look at the Franciscan Visitor Center sends an unmistakable message. The entire public area is all about the elements: the spectacular cascade of water in the courtyard fountain; the sun-baked sand exterior of the Spanish Mission–style building; the light pouring into the tasting room from a full-length clerestory window; and an oversized fireplace that heats the space right up to its vaulted ceiling. The airy feel of the well-lit interior is brought down to earth by the stone floor, sand-colored walls, dark wood display cases, and four-sided walnut tasting bar ringed with a zinc countertop. Large double doors lead to a walled terrace furnished with tables and chairs. At the back of the main tasting room, soaring glass doors open onto a spacious library, where more than three decades of the winery's history are on display—in bottles.

FRANCISCAN

CABERNET SAUVIGNON
VINTAGE 2004 • NAPA VALLEY

Franciscan dates to 1972, when it was founded by a group of San Francisco lawyers and doctors. Three years later, they sold the winery to Raymond Duncan and Justin Meyer, who also owned Silver Oak Cellars. In 1978 the brand and the estate vineyards were purchased by the Peter Eckes Company of Germany. In 1985, after Meyer returned to Silver Oak, the company found a new president in Agustin Huneeus, a Chilean who had built the Concha y Torra winery in his native country.

Huneeus quickly earned a reputation for innovation and leadership. He determined that the estate vineyard would reach its finest expression as a blend in the tradition of the great Bordeaux wines. In the 1980s, Franciscan debuted Magnificat, a hand-selected blend of the vintage's finest lots of fruit, predominantly Cabernet Sauvignon, with smaller percentages of Merlot, Malbec, and Cabernet Franc. At that time, however, American wines were identified by variety, not by place of origin, as is the practice in France. The laws did not allow Magnificat to be labeled as a Cabernet or Merlot, but it was clearly more than a mere table wine. So Huneeus gathered fellow vintners Robert Mondavi and Joseph Phelps, and the trio instigated a campaign to change the restrictive label laws and give winemakers the freedom to make the best wines they could. Their efforts resulted in a new term for these blends—Meritage (rhymes with heritage), a word that conveys their superior quality.

In 1987 Franciscan introduced Napa's first wild yeast–fermented Chardonnay. In lieu of commercial yeasts, Cuvée Sauvage is made with a mixture of wild strains, which work slowly and in concert to create layers of complexity in each barrel of wine.

Visitors can learn more about these and other Franciscan wines in a variety of in-depth sessions conducted in private, clublike rooms located off the library.

FRANK FAMILY VINEYARDS

At a time when many Napa Valley wineries are increasingly exclusive, the convivial, unpretentious ambience at Frank Family Vineyards is decidedly refreshing. What's more, the winery bucks another local trend by offering complimentary tastings. Yet these are not the main reasons for heading slightly off the beaten path to reach this historic property. The Frank Family Vineyards wines are made in a massive stone building first constructed in 1884 as Larkmead Winery. Refurbished in 1906 with sandstone from the nearby hills, the structure is listed on the National Register of Historic Places and as an official Point of Historical Interest in the state of California.

In 1992 Rich Frank, former president of Disney Studios, had the opportunity to purchase the Kornell Champagne Cellars at Lark-  mead Winery. A sentimental guy at heart, Frank continues to pro- duce sparkling wines in the old cellar where thick stone walls, high- stacked barrels, and the unmistakable bouquet of aging wines impart an almost palpable sense of history. Winemaker Todd Graff, who was pre- viously a winemaker at Schramsberg, handcrafts Blanc de Blancs, Blanc de Noirs, Rouge, and Reserve in the tra- ditional French *méthode champenoise* style. Visitors can see the equipment Graff uses to produce 2,200 cases of sparkling wine each year.

The focus at Frank Family Vineyards, however, is largely on still wines, using grapes from three distinguished Napa vineyards. Winston Hill, Rich Frank's personal estate, is situated five hundred feet above the valley floor in Rutherford and produces Cabernet Sauvignon as well as small amounts of Merlot, Cabernet Franc, and Sangiovese. The grapes from this vineyard are used for Frank Family's estate wines—Winston Hill Red Wine, Rutherford Reserve Cabernet, and Rutherford Sangiovese. Fruit for the winery's Napa Valley Cabernet Sauvignon also comes from Capell Valley, located east of the Vaca Range. Frank Family's vineyards at Buchli Station are in the heart of the Carneros, where the combination of cool maritime climate and shallow, dense clay loam soils produces lively, well-balanced Chardonnay and Pinot Noir.

The Frank Family Vineyards no-frills tasting room has remained virtually unchanged over the years. In a small residential-style structure adjacent to the winery, visitors are welcomed heartily and offered samples of sparkling wines. Those interested in tasting the still wines are ushered into the back room, where they are served five wines and can request a taste of something that may not be on that day's list of available wines. On the south side of the building, in the shade of oak trees as old as the winery, wooden picnic tables afford visitors a place to relax and enjoy the wonderful vineyard view.

FRANK FAMILY VINEYARDS
1091 Larkmead Ln.
Calistoga, CA 94515
800-574-9463
info@frankfamilyvineyards.
com
www.frankfamilyvineyards.
com

OWNER: Rich Frank.

LOCATION: About 1 mile north of St. Helena via Hwy. 29.

APPELLATION: Napa Valley.

HOURS: 10 A.M.–5 P.M. daily.

TASTINGS: Complimentary.

TOURS: By appointment.

THE WINES: Cabernet Sauvignon, Chardonnay, Pinot Noir, Sangiovese, sparkling wine, Zinfandel.

SPECIALTIES: Cabernet Sauvignon from Rutherford, Chardonnay, sparkling wine.

WINEMAKER: Todd Graff.

ANNUAL PRODUCTION: 20,000 cases.

OF SPECIAL NOTE: Reserve Chardonnay, Reserve Pinot Noir, Port, Sangiovese, and sparkling wines available only at winery.

NEARBY ATTRACTIONS: Bothe-Napa State Park; Robert Louis Stevenson State Park; Old Faithful Geyser of California; Petrified Forest; hot-air balloon rides; Sharpsteen Museum (exhibits on Robert Louis Stevenson and Walt Disney animator Ben Sharpsteen).

GRGICH HILLS CELLAR

GRGICH HILLS CELLAR
1829 St. Helena Hwy.
Rutherford, CA 94573
800-532-3057
info@grgich.com
www.grgich.com

OWNERS: Miljenko "Mike" Grgich and Austin Hills.

LOCATION: About 3 miles south of St. Helena.

APPELLATION: Napa Valley.

HOURS: 9:30 A.M.–4:30 P.M. daily.

TASTINGS: $10 for 5 wines.

TOURS: By appointment, 11 A.M. and 2 P.M. daily.

THE WINES: Cabernet Sauvignon, Chardonnay, Fumé Blanc, Merlot, Violetta (late-harvest dessert wine), Zinfandel.

SPECIALTY: Chardonnay.

WINEMAKER: Mike Grgich.

ANNUAL PRODUCTION: 80,000 cases.

OF SPECIAL NOTE: Barrel tastings held 2–4 P.M. on Friday afternoons in summer. Napa Valley Wine Train stops at Grgich Hills for special tour and tasting; call 800-427-4124 for schedule.

NEARBY ATTRACTIONS: Bothe-Napa State Park (hiking, picnicking, horseback riding, swimming Memorial Day–Labor Day); Bale Grist Mill State Historic Park (waterpowered mill circa 1846); Silverado Museum (Robert Louis Stevenson memorabilia).

Few people driving along Highway 29 recognize both of the red, white, and blue flags flying in front of this winery. They certainly know one, the American flag. The other represents Croatia, the native country of winemaker and co-owner Miljenko "Mike" Grgich.

The simple red-tile-roofed, white stucco building may not be as flashy as those of nearby wineries, but as the saying goes, it's what's inside that counts. Once visitors pass beneath the grapevine trellis and into the dimly lit recesses of the tasting room, they forget about exterior appearances. The comfortable, old-world atmosphere at Grgich Hills Cellar is not a gimmick.

The winery was founded by Mike Grgich (pronounced GUR-gitch) and Austin E. Hills on July 4, 1977. Both were already well known. Hills is a member of the Hills Brothers coffee family. Grgich was virtually notorious, especially in France. He had drawn worldwide attention in 1976, when, at the now-famous "Paris Tasting," an all-French panel of judges chose his 1973 Chateau Montelena Chardonnay over the best of the white Burgundies in a blind tasting.

It was a momentous occasion for the California wine industry in general and in particular for Mike Grgich, who was already acknowledged as one of the state's top winemakers.

Finally in a position to capitalize on his fame, Grgich quickly found a simpatico partner in Hills, who had a background in business and finance and was the owner of established vineyards. The two men shortly began turning out the intensely flavored Chardonnays that remain the flagship wines of Grgich Hills Cellar.

Grgich, easily recognizable with his trademark black beret, was born in 1923 into a winemaking family on the Dalmatian coast of Croatia. He arrived in California in 1958 and spent his early years at Beaulieu Vineyard, where he worked with the late, pioneering winemaker André Tchelistcheff before moving on to Mondavi and Chateau Montelena. Grgich continues to make wine and relies on a younger generation—daughter Violet Grgich, vice president of sales and marketing, and nephew Ivo Jeramaz, vice president of production and vineyard development—to carry on the family tradition. Visitors may well run into family members when taking the exceptionally informative winery tour or while sampling wines in the cool, cellarlike tasting room or in the newly built VIP tasting room and hospitality center.

HALL

Craig and Kathryn Hall have scarcely paused for breath since 2003, when they purchased an existing tasting room where they could share their wines—all Bordeaux varietals—with the public. Their first order of business was to remodel the old building, a small structure built in the 1980s, into an airy, color-filled space further brightened with original artwork from their personal collection.

The Halls commissioned several additional works, mostly wine-related sculptures such as *Baccus* (a figure eating grapes) and *Alpha* (a kinetic sculpture) that are displayed on the front and side walkways. The most imposing work in the entrance courtyard is a seven-foot-tall sculpture, *Moebus Tower*, by Texas artist Michelle O'Michael. Its form, a horizontal figure eight, represents the geometric symbol for infinity. Painted a vibrant red, it inspired the color of the winery's logo. Other contemporary pieces of sculpture adorn the tasting room and the lawn in back, where guests can relax in a sort of outdoor gallery with unimpeded views of the Mayacamas Range to the west. Extensive plantings of penstemon, lavender, miniature roses, and other perennials create a lush garden setting, especially around the arbor-covered courtyards.

The Hall estate in St. Helena also includes an irreplaceable piece of history: an original stone winery built in 1885 by New England sea captain William Peterson. The winery eventually passed through several owners, most notably the Napa Valley Cooperative Winery, a major producer in the 1930s. By the late twentieth century, the original winery was engulfed by the larger facility.

Visitors who make reservations for tours are ushered to the "historic winery" and offered barrel samples of future wines, an experience affording a lively contrast between the Old World and the new. That juxtaposition is destined to become dramatically more vivid in a few years. The Halls, who have long been planning to replace the former Napa co-op winery with a modern winemaking facility, also intend to restore and showcase the Peterson structure. To this end, they engaged renowned architect Frank Gehry to design the project, which is slated for completion in 2009.

Meanwhile, in 2005, the Halls completed a new production facility at their Rutherford winery that features high-tech fermentation tanks, a sophisticated gravity-flow system, and barrel cellars designed by Austrian cellar master Freiderich Gruber. Kathryn Hall, a former U.S. Ambassador to Austria, and her husband, Texas financier Craig Hall, own more than three thousand acres in Sonoma and Napa, of which five hundred acres are planted to vineyards.

HALL
St. Helena:
401 Hwy. 29 South
St. Helena, CA 94574
866-667-HALL (4255)
707-967-2620
Rutherford:
Rutherford, CA 94575
707-967-0700
info@hallwines.com
www.hallwines.com

OWNERS: Craig and Kathryn Hall.

LOCATION: St. Helena: 1.5 miles north of Rutherford; Rutherford: call for directions.

APPELLATION: Napa Valley.

HOURS: 10 A.M.–5:30 P.M. daily; Rutherford: by appointment.

TASTINGS: $10 for 3 wines.

TOURS: St. Helena: Historic Winery & Barrel Tasting by appointment ($20); Rutherford: by appointment, 10 A.M., 2 P.M., and 4 P.M. daily ($30).

THE WINES: Cabernet Franc, Cabernet Sauvignon, Merlot, Sauvignon Blanc.

SPECIALTY: Bordeaux varietals.

WINEMAKER: Richard Batchelor.

ANNUAL PRODUCTION: 15,000 cases.

OF SPECIAL NOTE: Shaded arbor at St. Helena with view of outdoor art collection. Many wines available only at winery.

NEARBY ATTRACTIONS: Bothe-Napa State Park (hiking, picnicking, horseback riding, swimming Memorial Day–Labor Day); Napa Valley Opera House (live performances in an historic building); Culinary Institute of America at Greystone (cooking demonstrations).

HEITZ WINE CELLARS

HEITZ WINE CELLARS
Tasting Room:
436 St. Helena Hwy. South
St. Helena, CA 94574
707-963-2047
Winery:
500 Taplin Rd.
St. Helena, CA 94574
707-963-3542
www.heitzcellar.com

OWNERS: Heitz family.

LOCATION: 2.5 miles south of
St. Helena (tasting room).

APPELLATION: Napa Valley.

HOURS: 11 A.M.–4:30 P.M.
daily (tasting room).

TASTINGS: Complimentary.

TOURS: Of winery by
appointment.

THE WINES: Cabernet
Sauvignon, Chardonnay,
Grignolino, Grignolino
Rosé, Port, Zinfandel.

SPECIALTY: Vineyard-
designated Cabernet
Sauvignons.

WINEMAKERS: David Heitz
and Joe Norman.

ANNUAL PRODUCTION:
38,000 cases.

OF SPECIAL NOTE: Only
producer of Italian variety
of Grignolino in Napa
Valley.

NEARBY ATTRACTIONS:
Bothe-Napa State Park
(hiking, picnicking, horse-
back riding, swimming
Memorial Day–Labor Day);
Bale Grist Mill State
Historic Park (water-
powered mill, circa 1846);
Culinary Institute of
America at Greystone
(cooking demonstrations);
Silverado Museum
(Robert Louis Stevenson
memorabilia).

Most travelers interested in sampling Heitz wines will visit the tasting room on Highway 29, the original site of the winery founded in 1961 by Joe and Alice Heitz. Palms, traditional symbols of hospitality, greet visitors turning off the highway toward the native-stone building that opened in 2002. Inside, the mahogany floors, cabinets, and long, low tasting bar make for a sophisticated space. Behind the tasting room is a patio with ample bench seating in the shade of a pergola. Just fifteen feet beyond it are the very first vineyards planted by the Heitzes.

Today, a second generation is in charge of Heitz Wine Cellars: president Kathleen Heitz Myers and her brother, winemaker David Heitz. David has earned accolades beginning with his first solo effort, in 1974. No one was surprised by his success, since David learned the wine business at the knee of his father, one of  the most influential winemakers of of his time. The late Joe Heitz honed his craft at a few wineries, notably Beaulieu Vineyard, where he spent seven years as under-study to acclaimed winemaker André Tchelistcheff.

It didn't take Joe and Alice Heitz long to outgrow their 8-acre property. In 1964 they relocated two miles east, to a 160-acre residence and ranch on Taplin Road, a tiny country road in an area known locally as Spring Valley. The original winery became the first tasting room, then was replaced by the structure visitors see today. The Taplin Road property had first been developed as a winery and vineyard in the 1880s by the Swiss-Italian family of Anton Rossi. Old oaks, rosebushes, wisteria, shaded benches, a couple of small farmhouses, and a beautiful 1898 stone cellar make parts of the ranch look more like a movie set than a working winery. Today, the Heitz family farms a total of 370 acres of vineyards at their various Napa Valley ranches.

The most famous wines Heitz makes come from three prestigious Napa Valley Cabernet vineyards: Martha's Vineyard, Trailside Vineyard, and Bella Oaks Vineyard. Perhaps no other vineyard name in the United States is as widely recognized as Martha's Vineyard in Oakville. Owned by the Tom and Martha May family, the thirty-four-acre property produces Cabernet Sauvignon known for its minty characteristics, rich flavors, and overall balance.

Like their parents before them, Kathleen Heitz Myers and David Heitz continue to nurture lasting relationships with their neighbors, placing a high premium on preserving the agricultural heritage of the Napa Valley. To that end, they practice sustainable and organic farming, which not only creates healthier vines, but also ensures that the distinct characteristics of each vineyard are expressed in the complexities of the wine.

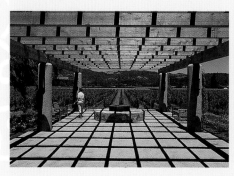

THE HESS COLLECTION WINERY

A gently winding road wends up a forested mountainside to this winery on the western rim of the Napa Valley. Although only a ten-minute drive from bustling Highway 29, the estate feels a thousand times removed. Arriving visitors are greeted with stunning vineyard views from almost every vantage point.

Swiss entrepreneur Donald Hess has owned vineyards on Mount Veeder since 1978, so when he decided to establish his own winery, he didn't have to look far to find the Christian Brothers Mont La Salle property. He already knew that the east side of the extinct volcano provides a cool climate that allows a long growing season as well as excellent soil drainage—two viticultural components known for producing grapes of aromas and flavors. Vine-land in the 1860s, long before winery was built in 1903. The wine here for nearly a half

with an intense concentration yards were first planted on this the three-story, ivy-clad stone Christian Brothers produced century before leasing the facilities to Hess in 1986. He began planting Chardonnay and Cabernet Sauvignon vineyards on terrain so steep they have to be picked by hand. The vines must grow extended roots to cling to the mountainside, and the resultant stress creates fruit of exceptional character.

The Hess Collection farms 315 acres of Mount Veeder vineyards that range in elevation from six hundred to two thousand feet. Viewing itself as a steward of the land, the winery farms these vineyards using the principles of sustainable and organic agriculture.

Hess spent two years renovating the facility before opening it to the public in 1989. The overhaul included transforming thirteen thousand square feet on the second and third floors to display his extensive collection of art, which includes 143 paintings, sculptures, and interactive pieces by modern and contemporary international artists including such luminaries as Francis Bacon, Frank Stella, Robert Rauschenberg, and Robert Motherwell. Two works evoke a particularly strong response for their social commentary. One is Argentinean Leopold Maler's *Hommage 1974*, an eternally burning typewriter created in protest of the repression of artistic freedom. Another is Polish sculptor Magdalena Abakanowicz's *Crowd*, a group of nineteen life-size headless figures made of resin and burlap sacks.

The tasting room, which shares the first floor with a century-old barrel-aging cellar, has one wall consisting of a local metamorphic sandstone called rhyolite. The stone had been covered with stucco by the Christian Brothers but was inadvertently exposed during the winery's renovation. This is where visitors linger and share their impressions of both the wine and the art.

THE HESS COLLECTION WINERY
4411 Redwood Rd.
Napa, CA 94558
707-255-1144, ext. 236
or 220
vcenter@hesscollection.com
www.hesscollection.com

OWNER: The Hess Group AG, Switzerland.

LOCATION: 7 miles west of Hwy. 29.

APPELLATION: Mount Veeder and Napa Valley.

HOURS: 10 A.M.–5 P.M. daily.

TASTINGS: : $10–$20. Food-and-wine pairings at 10 A.M. and 2 P.M. on Thursday, Friday, and Saturday by reservation.

TOURS: Collection open daily. Guided tours of winery and collection available.

THE WINES: Cabernet Sauvignon, Chardonnay, Mountain Cuvée, Petit Sirah, Sauvignon Blanc, Viognier, late-harvest Viognier, Zinfandel.

SPECIALTIES: Mount Veeder Cabernet Sauvignon, Chardonnay, Cuvée.

WINEMAKERS: David Guffy (Hess Collection and The Lion) and Randle Johnson (Artezin).

ANNUAL PRODUCTION: 90,000 cases.

OF SPECIAL NOTE: Extensive collection of international contemporary and modern art. Annual events include Spring Garden Party (April), Harvest Party (October), Holiday Open House (December). Many wines available only in tasting room.

NEARBY ATTRACTIONS: COPIA: The American Center for Wine, Food and the Arts; Alston Regional Park (hiking); Westwood Hills Regional Park (hiking).

MARKHAM VINEYARDS

MARKHAM VINEYARDS
2812 St. Helena Hwy. North
St. Helena, CA 94574
707-963-5292
www.markhamvineyards.
com

OWNER:
Mercian Corporation.

LOCATION: 1 mile north of
St. Helena on Hwy. 29.

APPELLATION: Napa Valley.

HOURS: 10 A.M.–5 P.M. daily.

TASTINGS: $5 for 4
premium wines; $8 for
4 hard-to-find wines;
$15 for library or
reserve wines.

TOURS: By appointment.

THE WINES: Cabernet
Sauvignon, Chardonnay,
Merlot, Petite Sirah,
Pinot Noir, Reserve
Merlot, Sauvignon
Blanc, Zinfandel.

SPECIALTIES: All wines.

WINEMAKER: Kimberlee
Jackson Nicholls.

ANNUAL PRODUCTION:
130,000 cases.

OF SPECIAL NOTE: Craft
exhibits, book signings,
and art exhibit openings
in summer months. Food-
and-wine-pairing sessions
($35). Dinner in Stone
Cellar by reservation.
Pinot Noir available only
at winery.

NEARBY ATTRACTIONS:
Bothe-Napa State Park
(hiking, picnicking, horse-
back riding, swimming
Memorial Day–Labor
Day); Bale Grist Mill State
Historic Park (water-
powered mill circa 1846);
Culinary Institute of
America at Greystone
(cooking demonstrations);
Silverado Museum
(Robert Louis Stevenson
memorabilia).

Few people are surprised to hear that Charles Krug, Schramsberg, and Sutter Home wineries were in business in 1874. Less widely known is that they were the only three wineries operating in the Napa Valley that year, when Jean Laurent founded the St. Helena winery that, less than a century later, would become known as Markham Vineyards.

Laurent, a Frenchman from Bordeaux, arrived in California in 1852, drawn by the lure of the 1849 Gold Rush. When his prospecting failed to pan out, he made his way to the city of Napa in 1868 and began growing vegetables. Laurent quickly assessed the high quality of the soil and, being from Bordeaux, realized the Napa Valley was ideally suited to grapevines. Six years later, he established the Laurent Winery in St. Helena. After Laurent died in 1890, the property changed hands a number of times. In 1977,

it was purchased by Bruce Markham, who had already acquired prime vineyard land on the Napa Valley floor, including 93 acres in Yount-ville once owned by Ingle-nook. By 1978, he had added the Calistoga Ranch at the headlands of the Napa River and the Oak Knoll Vineyard in the Oak Knoll District. Altogether, the Markham estate vineyards now cover 330 acres, including the most recent acquisition, Trubody Vineyards, west of Yountville in the center of the valley. These four areas have distinct microclimates that contribute to the complexity of the various wines produced by the winery.

In 1988, the winery and vineyard holdings were sold to Japan's oldest and largest wine company, Mercian Corporation. Despite these changes, many things have remained constant. The current owners have maintained the winery's dedication to producing ultrapremium wines sold at relatively modest prices. The first employee hired by Markham, Bryan Del Bondio, a native of Napa Valley from a family immersed in winemaking, is now president of Markham Vineyards. Jean Laurent's original stone cellar sits at the heart of the facility.

Stylistically, the winery combines both historic and modern elements, with its old stone and concrete facade, and its subdued red metal roofing supported by round wooden columns. Lily ponds flank the approach to the tasting room, and beyond them, orange and yellow canna lilies provide bursts of color when the plants bloom in spring and summer. The tasting room has an atrium with a large fireplace that warms the huge space on cold days. Displayed throughout are fine art and crafts, from blown-glass torches, to jewelry and Limoges boxes, to hand-decorated ceramic plates, urns, and candlesticks. One side of the tasting room is devoted to changing exhibits by noted artists.

MUMM NAPA

For connoisseurs of champagne, relaxing outdoors on a sunny day with a glass of bubbly, good friends, and a vineyard view may be the ultimate pleasure. This is obviously what the founders of Mumm Napa had in mind when they conceived of establishing a winery in North America that could produce a sparkling wine that would live up to Champagne standards.

In 1979, representatives of Champagne Mumm of France began quietly searching for the ideal location for a winery. So secretive was their project that they even had a code name for it: Project Lafayette. The point man was  the late Guy Devaux, a native of Epernay, the epicenter of France's Champagne district and an expert on *méthode* style of winemaking, the wine undergoes its bubble-producing fermentation in the very bottle from which it *champenoise*. In this French will be drunk. Devaux crisscrossed the United States for four years before settling on Napa Valley, the country's best-known appellation.

The best way to appreciate Mumm Napa is to start with a tour. The winery has a reputation for putting on one of the best in the business, covering the complicated steps necessary to get all those bubbles into each bottle. The best time of year to take the tour is during the harvest season, usually between mid-August and mid-October. However, there is a lot to see at any time of year, and conveniently, the entire tour takes place on one level.

Visitors enter the winery through the wine shop; the tasting veranda is just beyond, with spectacular views of the vineyards and the Mayacamas Range.

Mumm Napa is also noted for its commitment to fine art photography. The winery exhibits the work of many renowned, as well as local, photographers in its expansive galleries. Guests may explore the Photography Galleries at their leisure, even while they enjoy a glass of sparkling wine. Most notable is the private collection of Mathew Adams, grandson of photographer Ansel Adams, on display in the exhibition gallery.

MUMM NAPA
8445 Silverado Trail
Rutherford, CA 94573
707-967-7700
mumm_club@
mummnapa.com
www.mummnapa.com

OWNER: Pernod
Ricard USA.

LOCATION: East of
Rutherford, 1 mile south
of Rutherford Cross Rd.

APPELLATION: Napa Valley.

HOURS: 10 A.M.–5 P.M. daily.

TASTINGS: 3 half flutes
for $8 and up; $8–12 for
reserve wines.

TOURS: Hourly, 10 A.M.–
3 P.M.

THE WINES: Blanc de
Blancs, Blanc de Noirs,
Brut Prestige, Demi Sec,
DVX, Sparkling Pinot
Noir, Vintage Reserve.

SPECIALTY: Sparkling wine
made in traditional
French style.

WINEMAKER:
Ludovic Dervin.

ANNUAL PRODUCTION:
200,000 cases.

OF SPECIAL NOTE: Exhibits
of internationally known
and local photographers.
Limited availability of
Chardonnay, Pinot Gris,
and Pinot Noir, and
of large-format bottles,
at winery.

NEARBY ATTRACTIONS:
Napa Valley Museum
(winemaking displays,
art exhibits).

NICKEL & NICKEL

NICKEL & NICKEL
8164 Hwy. 29
Oakville, CA 94562
707-967-9600
info@nickelandnickel.com
www.nickelandnickel.com

OWNER:
Private partnership.

LOCATION: On Hwy. 29 just north of Oakville Crossroad.

APPELLATION: Oakville.

HOURS: 10 A.M.–3 P.M. Monday–Friday; 10 A.M.–2 P.M. Saturday–Sunday.

TASTINGS: By appointment. $30 for 5 wines.

TOURS: By appointment.

THE WINES: Cabernet Sauvignon, Chardonnay, Merlot, Syrah, Zinfandel.

SPECIALTY: 100 percent varietal, single-vineyard wines.

WINEMAKER: Darice Spinelli.

ANNUAL PRODUCTION: 30,000 cases.

OF SPECIAL NOTE: Restored 19th-century farmstead, including Queen Anne residence. Bottle limits on some wines.

NEARBY ATTRACTIONS: Napa Valley Museum (winemaking displays, art exhibits).

From the outside, the Nickel & Nickel winery is a charming, well-kept Napa Valley farm dating from the late nineteenth century. Yet, a closer look reveals that the farmstead facade camouflages a stunning, state-of-the-art winery that was designed exclusively to produce 100 percent varietal, single-vineyard wines.

Indeed, some of the buildings have been standing since the 1880s, when the surrounding land was settled by John C. Sullenger, the original landholder. This includes the stately farmhouse, featuring charming Queen Anne details, where visitors to Nickel & Nickel are welcomed. Restored in 2003 and named for its original owner, the Sullenger House is one of several restored buildings on the forty-two-acre estate that together capture the spirit of a nineteenth-century farm and create an architectural gem that mingles brand-new winemaking facilities with historic structures.

Visitors are met by the Sullenger House concierge and poured a glass of Chardonnay to enjoy in the living room. From the Sullenger House, the tour proceeds to the outbuildings where wine is made and stored. The only new building at Nickel & Nickel is the 5,800-square-foot fermentation barn, a post-and-beam structure fashioned from some 450 reclaimed, century-old fir beams. It was assembled using nineteenth-century techniques such as hand joinery for post-and-beam construction. From there, visitors are led down to the 30,000-square-foot underground cellar, which has groin arches and vaulted ceilings and can accommodate 3,200 French oak barrels.

The Sullenger House and farmstead buildings flank a traditional courtyard and are surrounded by eighty-year-old Sevillano olive trees and a white, three-rail fence. Extensive landscaping includes river birch, weeping willow, and Japanese maple trees, thirty-foot Canary palm trees, and a host of shrubs, perennials, and native plants. Guided sit-down tastings for a limited number of people are usually conducted in the dining room, or, depending on the time of year, tastings may also be held in the cellar, with its French tile floors and vaulted ceiling, or on the back porch.

The wine tastings include five of Nickel & Nickel's collection of 100 percent varietal, single-vineyard wines, all intended to express the distinct personality of each location. Except for a few select Sonoma vineyards, the wines come primarily from the Napa Valley. The sources range from eight acres in the Carpenter Vineyard in the Coombsville area of south Napa, to the small Dragonfly Vineyard in St. Helena, to thirty acres of clay loam soil in Sullenger Vineyard, the winery's home vineyard in Oakville.

PARADUXX WINERY

It is rare for any winery to offer side-by-side tastings of two, let alone three, vintages, but this practice is standard at the Paraduxx Vineyard House. The winery's tasting room opened in the fall of 2005 in a brand-new, mustard yellow building designed by the same San Francisco architectural firm—Baum Thornley—that is responsible for the Estate House at Duckhorn Vineyards in St. Helena.

Like the tasting room at the parent winery, the Vineyard House has classic farmhouse-style exterior elements artfully juxtaposed with thoroughly modern interior decor. Numerous picture windows and a skylight in the vaulted ceiling allow an abundance of natural light to bathe the room. Myriad seat-  ing options include a large square table in the middle, tufted black leather chairs and benches, square black and beige ottomans, and tall cocktail tables arranged along the walls. There are even window seats for those who want to soak up the vineyard views. Potted palms, chrome finishings, and a sisal rug edged in black complete the sleek, contemporary look.

The wine-tasting experience is as unconventional as the room itself. Once seated, visitors are handed trim black and chrome menus listing wines, Paraduxx logo merchandise, and prices. Then a staff member sets the table with a selection of small food pairings, a bottle of spring water, and a curvilinear chrome tray holding chic, stemless Riedel "O" crystal glasses nearly filled with wine. Visitors also receive postcard-size replicas of the original artist labels that include the winemaker's notes for each specially blended vintage.

Duckhorn Wine Company created the Paraduxx brand in 1994 to allow its winemakers to explore other styles without distracting from Duckhorn's focus on Bordeaux varietals. Zinfandel and Cabernet Sauvignon are the foundation of each unique blend, and any given vintage may also include Cabernet Franc or Merlot in its mix of Napa Valley mountain fruit and grapes from the surrounding estate vineyards. The Paraduxx property, which occupies a gentle slope from the Silverado Trail down to Rector Creek, is planted with Cabernet Sauvignon, Merlot, Cabernet Franc, and Zinfandel, in descending order. The winemaking is done in an unusual ten-sided fermentation building between the Vineyard House and Rector Creek.

For each vintage, Paraduxx commissions a different artist to create a work of art depicting a pair of ducks native to the Pacific Flyway. Each piece is transformed into duck stamp labels and applied to every bottle. All the works are displayed in the tasting room gallery. These depictions of nature scenes and wildlife befit the winery's setting amid stately redwood trees and understated landscaping.

PARADUXX WINERY
7257 Silverado Trail
Napa, CA 94558
707-945-0890
866-367-9943
tastings@paraduxx.com
www.paraduxx.com

OWNER: Duckhorn
Wine Company.

LOCATION: Between
Yountville Cross Rd. and
Oakville Cross Rd.

APPELLATION: Napa Valley.

HOURS: 11 A.M.–4 P.M. daily.

TASTINGS: By appointment.
$10 for 3 wines.

TOURS: None.

THE WINES:
Proprietary blends.

SPECIALTY:
Zinfandel–Cabernet
Sauvignon blends.

WINEMAKER:
Bill Nancarrow.

ANNUAL PRODUCTION:
12,000 cases.

OF SPECIAL NOTE:
Gallery displaying original
paintings created for the
winery's labels.

NEARBY ATTRACTIONS:
Napa Valley Museum
(winemaking displays,
art exhibits).

PEJU

PEJU
8466 Hwy. 29
Rutherford, CA 94573
707-963-3600
800-446-7358
info@peju.com
www.peju.com

OWNERS: Anthony and Herta Peju.

LOCATION: 10 miles north of town of Napa on Hwy. 29.

APPELLATION: Napa Valley.

HOURS: 10 A.M.–6 P.M. daily.

TASTINGS: $7 (applicable to wine purchase).

TOURS: Self-guided or by appointment.

THE WINES: Cabernet Franc, Cabernet Sauvignon, Chardonnay, Merlot, Provence, Sauvignon Blanc, Syrah, Zinfandel.

SPECIALTIES: Rutherford Reserve Cabernet, Cabernet Franc, and Carnival, a French Colombard.

WINEMAKER: Anthony Peju.

ANNUAL PRODUCTION: 35,000 cases.

OF SPECIAL NOTE: Grape Stomping Party (September). Lush gardens with fountains and sculpture. About 80 percent of wines available only at winery.

NEARBY ATTRACTIONS: Silverado Museum (Robert Louis Stevenson memorabilia); Napa Valley Museum (winemaking displays, art exhibits); Culinary Institute of America at Greystone (cooking demonstrations).

Spotting Peju, even on a winery-lined stretch of Highway 29, is easy, thanks to a fifty-foot-tall tasting tower topped with a distinctive patinated copper roof. Although the tasting tower opened only in late 2003, the structure already looks weathered, as if it has been there for decades. Like the rest of the property, it could have been transplanted directly from the countryside of southern France.

The Rutherford estate had been producing wine grapes for more than eighty years when Anthony and Herta Peju bought it in 1983. The couple have been improving the thirty-acre property ever since, streamlining vineyard techniques and adding Merlot and Cabernet Franc grapes to the estate's core product, Cabernet Sauvignon. By the mid-1990s, demand for Peju wines outstripped the winery's supply. To satisfy it, the Pejus acquired a 350-acre property in northern Napa County in the Pope Valley District, planted a variety of grapes, and named it Persephone Vineyard, after a goddess in Greek mythology.

The Pejus entered the wine business by a somewhat circuitous route. Anthony Peju had been living in Europe when he was lured to Los Angeles by the movie industry, but then became interested in horticulture. After he met Herta Behensky, his future wife, he established his own nursery, yet secretly dreamed of owning a farm. The vibrant towns of the Napa Valley and their proximity to San Francisco's cultural attractions enticed him to search for vineyard property. A two-year quest ended in the purchase of what would become Peju Province Winery.

Peju's horticultural experience, combined with his wife's talent for gardening, resulted in two acres of immaculately kept winery gardens. Together, they established a dramatic series of outdoor rooms linked by footpaths and punctuated with fountains and marble sculpture. Hundreds of flowering plants and trees create an aromatic retreat for the Pejus and their visitors. Lining both sides of the driveway are forty-foot-tall sycamore trees, their trunks adorned by gnarled spirals. Anthony Peju has trained the trees over the years. They will eventually create a living arch so that visitors will feel they are approaching the winery through a tunnel of green. Visitors reach the tasting room by crossing a small bridge over a koi-filled pool with fountains. An entrance door of Brazilian cherrywood is carved with the image of a farm girl blending water and wine. Inside the room, three muses gaze down from a century-old stained-glass window. This and an enormous seven-light chandelier illuminate the Turkish tile floors and the copper-and-steel railing that leads to the mezzanine, where a strategically placed circular window offers a garden view.

PROVENANCE VINEYARDS

PROVENANCE VINEYARDS
1695 Hwy. 29
P.O. Box 668
Rutherford, CA 94573
707-968-3633
info@provenancevineyards.com
www.provenancevineyards.com

OWNER: Diageo Chateau & Estate Wines.

LOCATION: About 3 miles south of St. Helena.

APPELLATION: Rutherford.

HOURS: 10 A.M.–4 P.M. daily.

TASTINGS: $10 for 5 wines.

TOURS: None.

THE WINES: Cabernet Sauvignon, Merlot, Sauvignon Blanc.

SPECIALTY: Rutherford Cabernet Sauvignon.

WINEMAKER: Tom Rinaldi.

ANNUAL PRODUCTION: 55,000 cases.

OF SPECIAL NOTE: Display of artwork by local artists.

NEARBY ATTRACTIONS: Bothe-Napa State Park (hiking, picnicking, horseback riding, swimming Memorial Day–Labor day); Bale Grist Mill State Historic Park (water-powered mill circa 1846); Culinary Institute of America at Greystone (cooking demonstrations); Silverado Museum (Robert Louis Stevenson memorabilia).

The grapes for Provenance's Rutherford Cabernet Sauvignon come from a vineyard that is part of the old Caymus Ranchero, which belonged to George Yount and, later, Thomas Rutherford. One of the area's earliest settlers, Yount arrived in 1838 and is believed to have been the first to plant wine grapes in Napa Valley. Nearby Yountville is named for him, just as Rutherford is named for Thomas Rutherford, who married one of Yount's granddaughters and received a portion of the ranch as a wedding present.

The property continued to change notable hands. Georges de Latour, founder of Beaulieu Vineyard, bought the vineyard in the early 1900s, and decades later, in 1988, well-known grape grower Andy Beckstoffer purchased it and proceeded to replant it with grapevines better suited to the local soil and growing conditions. It is a prized parcel, not simply because of its history but especially because of Rutherford's enviable loamy soil and a growing season characterized by hot, cloudless days and fog-cooled mornings and evenings.

Having chosen these premium grapes as the focus of its production, the founders of Provenance sought a facility in Rutherford. When a forty-five-acre property formerly occupied by another winery became available in the summer of 2002, they did not hesitate to snap it up. Founding winemaker is Tom Rinaldi, who had spent twenty-two years making wine at Duckhorn Vineyards. At Provenance, he crafts Cabernet Sauvignon and Merlot for his longtime fans, using grapes from Napa's best sub-appellations for red wines.

By the time Provenance opened its doors in late 2003, the winemaking facility sported a fresh coat of Burgundy red paint, and the tasting room had been completely rebuilt. The first feature that visitors notice in the tasting room is the floor. It is made of old staves from barrels—more than nine hundred were used—which still bear legible cooper's marks. Lots of bare wood—on the walls and ceiling—and a horseshoe-shaped wood tasting bar create a clean look in keeping with the winery's displays of artwork by local artists. The white beamed ceiling and museum-quality lighting give the room the appearance of an art gallery.

The link between wine and art is underscored in the winery's name. *Provenance,* which rhymes with *Renaissance,* comes from a French term meaning "origin" or "source." In the world of art, connoisseurs rely on provenance, the record of an artwork's ownership since its creation, as a guarantee of authenticity. At Provenance, the legacy of the vineyards and the quality of the aesthetics attest to the authenticity of both the wine and the art.

ROBERT MONDAVI WINERY

ROBERT MONDAVI WINERY
7801 Hwy. 29
Oakville, CA 94562
707-259-9463
888-766-6328
info@robertmondavi
winery.com
www.robertmondaviwinery.
com

LOCATION: About 16 miles
north of the town of Napa.

APPELLATIONS: Oakville and
Napa Valley.

HOURS: 10 A.M.–5 P.M. daily.

TASTINGS: $5 for 1 wine in
Le Marche tasting room;
$30 for 5 wines or à la carte
in To Kalon tasting room.

TOURS: To Kalon tour
every hour by reservation
($25); other tours available
seasonally.

THE WINES: Cabernet
Sauvignon, Chardonnay,
Fumé Blanc, Merlot, Pinot
Noir, Sauvignon Blanc.

SPECIALTIES: Cabernet
Sauvignon Reserve and
Fumé Blanc Reserve.

WINEMAKER:
Genevieve Janssens.

ANNUAL PRODUCTION:
Unavailable.

OF SPECIAL NOTE: Extensive
tours, guided tastings, and
food-and-wine pairings,
some requiring reservations.
Cave visits and picnic area
available by tour only. Large
shop with wine books and
Italian imports. Summer
Festival Concert Series
(July–August); Cabernet
Sauvignon Reserve Release
Party (October).

NEARBY ATTRACTIONS: Napa
Valley Museum (displays
on winemaking and both
permanent and temporary
art exhibits); COPIA: The
American Center for Wine,
Food and the Arts.

Wineries come and wineries go in the Napa Valley, but in this fast-paced, high-stakes world, few can challenge the lasting achievements of the Robert Mondavi Winery. Since its inception forty years ago, it has remained in the forefront of innovation, from the use of cold fermentation, stainless steel tanks, and small French oak barrels to the collaboration with NASA employing aerial imaging to reveal the health and vigor of grapevines.

Founder Robert Mondavi's cherished goal of producing wines on a par with the best in the world made his name virtually synonymous with California winemaking. That vision is being carried out today with ambitious programs such as the recent To Kalon Project. Named after the historic estate vineyard surrounding the winery, this extensive renovation led to the 2000 unveiling of the To Kalon Fermentation Cellar, which capitalizes on the natural flow of gravity to transport wine through the production system. Although Robert Mondavi pioneered the use of stainless steel fermentation in the 1960s, To Kalon has returned to traditional oak fermentation, based on the belief that the use of oak enhances the aromas, flavors, and complexity of the winery's reserve, district, and vineyard-designated Cabernet Sauvignon.

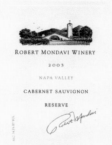

ROBERT MONDAVI WINERY
2003
NAPA VALLEY
CABERNET SAUVIGNON
RESERVE

Technological advances aside, the best reason for visiting Robert Mondavi Winery is something less tangible: an opportunity to experience the presentation of wine in the broader context of lifestyle. Educational tours and tastings, concerts, art exhibits, and the industry's first culinary program are all part of the Mondavi legacy. One of the most popular offerings is the To Kalon tour and tasting, which follows the path of the grape from the vine through the cellar to the finished wine. The 550-acre vineyard was named To Kalon (Greek for "the beautiful") by Hamilton Walker Crabb, a winegrowing pioneer who established vineyards here in the late 1800s. It was this property that inspired Robert Mondavi to establish his winery on the site.

Just as the estate's grapes express their *terroir* (the place where they are grown), the winery itself reflects the location and legacy of the Napa Valley. The Spanish mission-style architecture, with its expansive archway and bell tower designed by Clifford May, pays homage to the Franciscan fathers who planted the first grapes in the region. Two long wings project from the open-air lobby to embrace a wide expanse of lawn framed by the Mayacamas Range on the western horizon. Typical of the winery's commitment to the arts, several sculptures by regional artist Beniamino Benvenuto Bufano (who, like Robert Mondavi's family, came from Italy) are displayed in the courtyard and elsewhere around the grounds. In addition, the winery features art exhibits that change every two months.

ROMBAUER VINEYARDS

ROMBAUER VINEYARDS
3522 Silverado Trail
St. Helena, CA 94574
800-622-2206
707-963-5170
www.rombauervineyards.
com

OWNER:
Koerner Rombauer.

LOCATION: 1.5 miles north
of Deer Park Rd.

APPELLATION: Napa Valley.

HOURS: 10 A.M.–5 P.M. daily.

TASTINGS: Complimentary,
by appointment.

TOURS: By appointment.

THE WINES: Cabernet
Sauvignon, Chardonnay,
Merlot, Zinfandel.

SPECIALTY: Diamond
Selection Cabernet
Sauvignon.

WINEMAKER:
Gregory Graham.

ANNUAL PRODUCTION:
50,000 cases.

OF SPECIAL NOTE: Tours
include visit to barrel-
aging cellar. Copies of the
latest edition of *The Joy of
Cooking* and other cook-
books by Irma Rombauer
are available in the tasting
room. Zinfandel, Port,
and Joy, a late-harvest
Chardonnay, available
only at winery.

NEARBY ATTRACTIONS:
Bothe-Napa State Park
(hiking, picnicking, horse-
back riding, swimming
Memorial Day–Labor
Day); Silverado Museum
(Robert Louis Stevenson
memorabilia); Culinary
Institute of America at
Greystone (cooking
demonstrations).

The quarter-mile-long drive from the Silverado Trail leads to a winery ensconced in a forest of pine trees. On the far side of the low-slung building, a wide California ranch-style porch affords views that extend to the tree-covered ridge of the Mayacamas Range to the southeast. Without another structure in sight, the serene setting has the ambience of a fairytale kingdom secluded from the hustle and bustle of the valley floor. Directly below the winery, a gravel path winds down to a hill where roses are planted in the sun and azaleas thrive in the shade. Scattered about are a half-dozen metal sculptures of fantastical creatures such as a diminutive dinosaur and a life-size winged horse, all weathered to the point that they blend into the landscape.

The Rombauer family traces its heritage to another fertile wine area, the Rheingau region in Germany, where Koerner Rombauer's ancestors made wine. His great-aunt Irma Rombauer wrote the classic book *The Joy of Cooking*. The tradition of linking wine to food is carried on today, with every member of the family involved in the daily operation of the winery, from selecting grapes to marketing the final product. K. R. (Koerner Rombauer III) and his sister, Sheana, are now in charge, respectively, of national sales and public relations.

Koerner Rombauer, a former commercial airline captain, and his late wife, Joan, met and married in Southern California, where both had grown up in an agricultural environment. Since they had always wanted their children to have rural childhood experiences similar to their own, they came to the Napa Valley in search of land. In 1972, they bought fifty acres and settled into a home just up the hill from where the winery sits today. Within a few years, they became partners in a nearby winery. Their hands-on involvement in the winery's operations whetted their appetite for a label of their own and for making handcrafted wines with the passion and commitment of the family tradition. Taking advantage of the topography, the Rombauers built their family winery into the side of the hill. Rombauer Vineyards was completed in 1982.

By the early 1990s, the Rombauers realized they had the perfect location for excavating wine storage caves. Completed in 1997, the double-horseshoe-shaped cellar, extends for more than a mile into the hillside. Tours begin in the tasting room, which is personalized with an eclectic assortment of memorabilia from Koerner Rombauer's life. Among the more interesting items are the many signed photographs of famous people as diverse as test pilot Chuck Yeager, entertainer Barbra Streisand, former Secretary of State George Shultz, and country music star Garth Brooks, many of them with personal notes to Rombauer.

RUBICON ESTATE

RUBICON ESTATE
1991 St. Helena Hwy.
Rutherford, CA 94573
707-968-1100
800-RUBICON
tours@rubiconestate.com
www.rubiconestate.com

OWNERS: Francis and
Eleanor Coppola.

LOCATION: About 3 miles
south of St. Helena.

APPELLATIONS: Rutherford
and Napa Valley.

HOURS: 10 A.M.–5 P.M. daily;
until 6 P.M. Friday–Saturday,
Memorial Day–Labor Day.

TASTING: $25 guest fee
includes tasting of
5 estate wines.

TOURS: $15–45
(707-968-1161).

THE WINES: Blancaneaux
(white blend), Cabernet
Franc, Cabernet Sauvi-
gnon, Merlot, Rubicon
(red blend), Syrah,
Zinfandel.

SPECIALTY: Rubicon.

WINEMAKER: Scott McLeod.

ANNUAL PRODUCTION:
Unavailable.

OF SPECIAL NOTE: Historic
wine and film memorabilia
on display. Extensive
shop with gourmet
foods, books, and wine
and kitchen accessories.
More than 200 acres
of organically certified
vineyards.

NEARBY ATTRACTIONS:
Silverado Museum
(Robert Louis Stevenson
memorabilia); Napa Valley
Museum (winemaking
displays, art exhibits).

Academy Award–winning filmmaker Francis Ford Coppola and his wife, Eleanor, started making wine at the old Niebaum estate in 1975. Twenty years later, they bought the winery as well as the nineteenth-century château and adjacent vineyards. Flash back to 1879, when Gustave Niebaum, a Finnish sea captain, invested the fortune he acquired in the Alaska fur trade to establish his own winery, Inglenook. He modeled the massive stone château on the estates he had visited in Bordeaux. By the time the Coppolas entered the picture, however, a series of corporate ownerships had left the estate bereft of its reputation, its label, and much of its vineyard land.

The Coppolas reunited the major parcels of the original estate, which they named Niebaum-Coppola, and began restoring and  renovating the château and its grounds to their former glory. The European-style front courtyard now features a redwood and stone pergola graced with grapevines. Nearby, a ninety-by-thirty-foot reflecting pool is illuminated at night. In the vaulted entrance is one of Francis Coppola's most dramatic creations, a grand staircase built of exotic hardwoods imported from Belize. The Coppolas also mounted exhibits celebrating milestones in Inglenook's long, illustrious history.

When Francis Coppola set out to craft a proprietary red wine using the acclaimed estate vineyards, he found "the crossing of the Rubicon," Caesar's march on Rome, to be an appropriate metaphor in its implied "point of no return." So it was fitting that he renamed the winery Rubicon Estate in 2006, when the winery introduced profound changes to its image in general and its visitor programs in particular. In the past, thousands of people simply dropped in and wandered around the estate on their own, maybe staying for a tasting or to browse the extraordinary gift shop. To offer a more streamlined, personalized experience, the Coppolas decided to increase the emphasis on wine and education. To that end, visitors are charged a guest fee, good for three days, that entitles them to valet parking, access to the château, and a standard tasting of five estate wines.

Visitors seeking a more in-depth experience may sign up for any of several options: a guided walk in the estate vineyards; a historic tour of the château; a barrel sampling in the cellar; or an exploration of the flavors and aromas of selected wines. All of the tours include wine tasting. The most extensive offering, called Clone #29 after the estate's historic grape clone, begins in the vineyards, proceeds with a session on winemaking, and concludes with a private seated tasting of Rubicon paired with artisanal cheeses in a wing of the Infinity Cave, part of a sixteen-thousand-square-foot aging cellar completed in 2005.

Welcome to
RUTHERFORD
HILL

Cave Tours · Tasting · Sales   Daily from 10 to 5

RUTHERFORD HILL WINERY

RUTHERFORD HILL WINERY
200 Rutherford Hill Rd.
Rutherford, CA 94573
707-963-1871
info@rutherfordhill.com
www.rutherfordhill.com

OWNER: Terlato Wine Group.

LOCATION: About 2 miles south of St. Helena, just north of Rutherford Cross Rd. off Silverado Trail.

APPELLATION: Napa Valley.

HOURS: 10 A.M.–5 P.M. daily.

TASTINGS: $5 for 5 wines and logo glass; $10 for 5 reserve wines and logo glass.

TOURS: 11:30 A.M., 1:30 P.M., and 3:30 P.M. ($10); includes tasting of 5 wines and logo glass.

THE WINES: Cabernet Franc, Cabernet Sauvignon, Chardonnay, Malbec, Merlot, Petite Verdot, Rosé of Merlot, Sangiovese, Sauvignon Blanc.

SPECIALTIES: Cabernet Sauvignon, Chardonnay, Merlot.

WINEMAKER: Douglas Fletcher, director of winemaking.

ANNUAL PRODUCTION: 75,000 cases.

OF SPECIAL NOTE: Picnic areas with valley views. Wine-blending seminars. Rutherford Hill olive oil sold at winery. Caves available for private rental. Some limited-production wines sold only at winery.

NEARBY ATTRACTIONS: Auberge du Soleil (hotel, restaurant); Silverado Museum (Robert Louis Stevenson memorabilia).

Deep in a hillside east of the Silverado Trail lies a labyrinth of caves that extends nearly a mile. This subterranean facility is well suited for stashing thousands of barrels of wine that can age at fifty-eight to sixty degrees Fahrenheit and 85 percent humidity—ideal conditions for storing wine without the risk of evaporation that would occur in a less-humid environment. When the outside temperature spikes into the hundreds, all it takes is a major hosing down to set things right again.

A walk in the caves, which are redolent of red-wine aromas mingled with French and American oak, is a high point of a tour at Rutherford Hill. Built in 1984 at a cost of $1 million, the caves cover forty-four thousand square feet.  They were the first ones in the Napa Valley created with mining technology rather than the hand labor used at other wineries during the nineteenth century. Rutherford Hill is reached by a narrow road leading up from the Silverado Trail to a dead end in front of what looks like an ultra-deluxe barn. The large redwood structure has a steep-sloping roof that extends nearly to the ground. Rough-hewn external support beams anchor it in the so-called Rutherford dust. Outside the tasting room, a dramatic two-story arbor of wisteria vines partially shades a large sunken courtyard in springtime. It was the Rutherford dust that attracted a series of owners who realized the fine, rust-colored soil bore similarities to that of Bordeaux's Pomerol region, home to some of the world's finest Merlot.

The "barn," built by renowned winemaker Joseph Phelps, houses the winery and tasting room. In 1976, the property was purchased by Bill Jaeger, whose late wife, Lila, was a pioneer in initiating Napa's olive oil craze. Olive oil is still made from the trees on the winery property. Jaeger converted the forty-acre vineyard on the hill below the winery to Merlot vines, which continue to produce grapes for the current owner, Anthony Terlato, who took over in 1996. Terlato and his family, realizing that growing their own grapes would be the key to creating consistently complex, high-quality wines, subsequently purchased 60 additional acres in the Rutherford District and also farm another 130 Napa acres under long-term contracts.

The Terlato family's involvement in the wine business began with Anthony's father, who owned one of Chicago's largest wine stores. Over time, Anthony Terlato became a leading importer and marketer of fine wines from around the world, including those from Rutherford Hill. Having their own winery was the next logical step in the family's marrying of smart business and the pleasures of a wine country lifestyle.

SILVER OAK CELLARS

Fans of fine Cabernet Sauvignon line up hours in advance—sometimes even camping overnight—for the new release of each Silver Oak wine. The vigil has become something of a ritual for connoisseurs who want to be sure to take home some of the winery's hard-to-find bottles. During the early 1990s, on each semiannual release day in Napa Valley, just a handful of people waited for the winery doors to open, but as news of the extraordinary wine spread and the crowds grew larger, Silver Oak began serving espresso drinks and doughnuts to the early-morning crowds and passing hot hors d'oeuvres throughout the afternoon. Now each release day unfolds at both of the winery's estates, in Napa Valley and Alexander Valley, and many wine lovers plan vacations around the festive events.

The biggest attraction, of course, is what lies in the bottle. Silver Oak produces elegant Cabernet Sauvignons with fully developed flavors and seamless textures. The winemaking program combines meticulous vineyard practices, harmonious blending, and extensive aging in exclusively American oak barrels—followed by even more aging in bottles. When the wine reaches the consumer, it is a synergy of depth and delicacy.

The success of Silver Oak Cellars began with two visionary men, Ray Duncan and Justin Meyer. Duncan was an entrepreneur in Colorado before being lured to California in the 1960s to help a friend work on a vineyard deal. Impressed with the potential for wines in the Napa Valley and the Alexander Valley in Sonoma County, he purchased 750 acres of pastures, orchards, and vineyards within a year. In 1972, he formed a partnership with Meyer, a former Christian Brothers winemaker. The partners' work together lasted thirty years, until Meyer passed away in 2002.

Today the Duncan family sustains the commitment to excellence that has long been a hallmark of Silver Oak Cellars. Each of the two estates is devoted to an individual style of Cabernet Sauvignon. The Alexander Valley wine has a particularly soft and fruity character, while the somewhat bolder Napa Valley wine has firmer tannins, making it appropriate for longer cellar aging. Both estates welcome visitors and have tasting rooms where they can taste and compare the current release from each appellation. The Napa Valley winery, on the site of the old Keig Dairy in Oakville, features a massive stone building with a simple, but elegant, wood-paneled tasting room. The Alexander Valley winery has an airy tasting room and an inviting courtyard for relaxing and enjoying the leisurely pace of Sonoma County.

SILVER OAK CELLARS
Napa Valley:
915 Oakville Cross Rd.
Oakville, CA 94562
Alexander Valley:
24625 Chianti Rd.
Geyserville, CA 95441
800-273-8809
info@silveroak.com
www.silveroak.com

OWNER:
Raymond T. Duncan.

LOCATION: Napa Valley:
1.2 miles east of Hwy 29;
Alexander Valley: 7 miles
from Canyon Rd. exit off
U.S. 101 via Chianti Rd.

APPELLATIONS: Napa Valley
and Alexander Valley.

HOURS: 9 A.M.–4 P.M.
Monday–Saturday.

TASTINGS: $10 (complimentary glass included).
No reservations required.

TOURS: Monday–Friday,
1:30 P.M.; reservations
recommended.

THE WINE:
Cabernet Sauvignon.

SPECIALTY:
Cabernet Sauvignon.

WINEMAKER:
Daniel Baron.

ANNUAL PRODUCTION:
70,000 cases.

OF SPECIAL NOTE: Release
days are held simultaneously at both estates for
each wine: Napa Valley
Cabernet on the first
Saturday in February;
Alexander Valley Cabernet
on the first Saturday in
August. Purchase limits
on some vintages.

NEARBY ATTRACTIONS:
Napa Valley Museum
(winemaking displays,
art exhibits).

SILVERADO VINEYARDS

A steep, curving driveway, worthy of a ski slope, leads to the spectacular site of Silverado Vineyards. On either side of the road, wildflowers cling to the hillside as if for dear life. Yet nothing compares to the dramatic site of the winery itself, a vision in ocher and terra-cotta, stone and stucco, that brings Tuscany to mind. Many a visitor has noticed that Napa bears more than a passing resemblance to the Italian countryside.

In the mid-1970s, Diane Miller and her husband, Ron Miller, purchased two neighboring Napa Valley vineyards. "It was a a land that was working." For the grapes to local vintners, who made them. Inspired by this success, they 1981 and started construction on the public for tours and tastings in winery after the long-vanished min- on the slopes of nearby Mount St.

beautiful land," she says, "and it was first few years, the Millers sold their gold-medal-winning wines from established Silverado Vineyards in their own winery, which opened to 1987. The Millers named their new ing community that once thrived Helena. The name Silverado was made famous by author Robert Louis Stevenson, who lived there in the 1880s and wrote about the region in *The Silverado Squatters*.

Since Silverado was founded, the winery has acquired additional vineyards that it farms itself. Some, notably ninety-five acres of Cabernet Sauvignon and Merlot, are visible from the second-floor tasting room. Guests can sip their wine on a terrace paved with cobblestones that once graced New York City streets. If you look closely, you can see that some of the stones are worn smooth, while others are set bottom up, with their still-rough surfaces showing. Only a low wall separates the terrace from the abundant vines and wildflowers that bloom throughout the seasons.

The adjacent, spacious tasting room opened in 2000, replacing the much smaller original tasting room in another part of the building. French doors offer north-facing panoramas of vineyards and the hilly Stags Leap landscape. Huge antique beams of Douglas fir, imported from a lumber mill in British Columbia, span the ceiling. Overall, the design is grand but simple, recalling a Tuscan villa. Across the hall, double doors provide a view of a temperature-controlled barrel cellar. There is no access to the cellar from here, but visitors are invited to open the doors and inhale the heady aroma.

Visitors looking for an intimate Napa wine country experience will want to make reservations for one of Silverado's educational tastings and vineyard tours. The library tasting, limited to six participants, features four Cabernet Sauvignons of different vintages, paired with food, graciously presented in a breathtaking setting.

SILVERADO VINEYARDS
6121 Silverado Trail
Napa, CA 94575
707-257-1770
info@silveradovineyards.com
www.silveradovineyards.com

OWNERS: Miller family.

LOCATION: About 2 miles east of Yountville.

APPELLATION: Napa Valley.

HOURS: 10 A.M.–4:30 P.M. daily.

TASTINGS: $10 for 4 estate wines; $20 for reserve wines. Library tasting with food pairing by appointment.

TOURS: Of winery and vineyard by appointment.

THE WINES: Cabernet Sauvignon, Chardonnay, Merlot, Sangiovese, Sauvignon Blanc.

SPECIALTY: Solo Stags Leap Cabernet Sauvignon.

WINEMAKER: Jon Emmerich.

ANNUAL PRODUCTION: Unavailable.

OF SPECIAL NOTE: Limited-production wines available only in tasting room.

NEARBY ATTRACTIONS: Napa Valley Museum (winemaking displays, art exhibits); COPIA: The American Center for Wine, Food and the Arts.

SPRING MOUNTAIN VINEYARD

SPRING MOUNTAIN VINEYARD
2805 Spring Mountain Rd.
St. Helena, CA 94574
707-967-4188
office@springmtn.com
www.springmountain
vineyard.com

OWNER: J. E. Safra.

LOCATION: About 1.5 miles northwest of downtown St. Helena.

APPELLATION: Spring Mountain District.

HOURS: 10 A.M.–4 P.M. daily.

TASTINGS: By appointment.

TOURS: By appointment.

THE WINES: Estate-bottled Cabernet Sauvignon, Pinot Noir, Sauvignon Blanc, Syrah.

SPECIALTIES: Elivette Reserve Cabernet, mountain-grown Cabernet Sauvignon.

WINEMAKER: Jac Cole.

ANNUAL PRODUCTION: 10,000 cases.

OF SPECIAL NOTE: Tour includes visit to winery's extensive caves. Demonstration vineyard with gobelet trellising system. Displays of photography and antique farm equipment. Library selections of Cabernet Sauvignon.

NEARBY ATTRACTIONS: Bothe-Napa State Park (hiking, picnicking, horseback riding, swimming Memorial Day–Labor Day); Bale Grist Mill State Historic Park (waterpowered mill circa 1846); Culinary Institute of America at Greystone (cooking demonstrations); Silverado Museum (Robert Louis Stevenson memorabilia).

Every tour of the historic Spring Mountain Vineyard concludes with a sit-down wine tasting in a picturesque 1885 Victorian called Miravalle. The crowning glory of the Miravalle estate, this eight-thousand-square-foot mansion was built by the original owner, Tiburcio Parrott, one of the most colorful of Napa Valley's many nineteenth-century characters. The winery closed to the public in 1992 so that the owner could focus on restoration and replanting the hillside vineyards. It reopened in late 2003. The cream-colored mansion capped with a cupola boasts original ceilings, moldings, and inlaid wood floors. Another notable original feature is the stained-glass window with the bright green parrot on the first-floor landing. It may look familiar because the mansion was the fictional vintner's home on *Falcon Crest,* the popular 1980s television series.

The estate's real history is far more memorable than any soap opera. Spring Mountain Vineyard incorporates three properties that were producing wine in the late 1800s: Miravalle, Chateau Chevalier, and La Perla, site of the first Cabernet Sauvignon planting on Spring Mountain, in 1870. Even back then, grape growers and winemakers recognized the distinctive attributes of what is now known as the Spring Mountain District, namely, steep slopes and shallow soils that create such widely diverse conditions that Spring Mountain Vineyard has 135 identifiable vineyard blocks, each with a different elevation, exposure, and soil. Only 225 acres of the 845-acre estate have been planted—85 percent of them in classic red Bordeaux varieties: Cabernet Sauvignon, Cabernet Franc, Merlot, and Petit Verdot. Each year the winemaker captures the personality of the Spring Mountain Vineyard and the vintage in two blends, the Estate Cabernet Sauvignon and the reserve blend, Elivette.

Over the past 120 years, the property has been maintained or restored to look much as it did in the nineteenth century. Parrott had planted some six thousand olive trees and hundreds of citrus trees and roses. To these, the current owner added dozens of banana, fig, palm, and exotic fruit trees. A tour also includes an elegant old shingled horse barn with a collection of antique winemaking equipment and other historical objects. A gallery displays photographs of wine pioneers, including Tiburcio Parrott. Near the barn is a demonstration vineyard where visitors can view the winery's unusual "vertical gobelet" trellising system. Following this ancient method, each vine is shaped into a graceful goblet form resembling the glasses used for tasting red wines at Miravalle.

STERLING VINEYARDS

Travelers in the upper Napa Valley often get out their cameras as soon as they see the striking white buildings atop a three-hundred-foot forested knoll south of Calistoga. Even more camera-worthy is the journey to the winery via aerial tram. Cars and worries are left behind as visitors glide up the hill. The winery's designer, inspired by Napa's Mediterranean climate, intentionally modeled Sterling on the style of architecture on the photogenic Greek island of Mykonos.

The winery also stands out for its self-guided tours, which allow visitors to explore the facility from elevated platforms that feature educational graphics and a DVD video showing the entire winemaking process. The tour culminates on a  terrace offering a commanding view of the Napa Valley. Upon entering the main tasting room, guests are greeted with a complimentary glass of Sauvignon Blanc, then are shown to a table where the staff serves a choice of current releases. Visitors can enjoy the comfortable surroundings, or in warm weather sit on a patio with a view of the Bay Area's highest mountain, 4,344-foot Mt. St. Helena. New to the winery's hospitality offerings are the daily Reserve Tours, limited to eight participants, who are given a private tour that culminates in a guided tasting of three Cabernet Sauvignons.

Sterling was established in 1969 with the purchase of fifty vineyard acres by Englishman and international paper broker Peter Newton. In 2002, the winery completed a $14 million renovation, which included three new tasting rooms—one for the public, another for reserve wines, and yet another for Cellar Club members. Sterling has purchased a number of vineyards over the decades and now farms twelve hundred acres in the Napa Valley. These properties vary widely in topography, soil types, and microclimates, from the very steep Diamond Mountain Ranch west of Calistoga to the rolling hills around Winery Lake in the southern Carneros near San Francisco Bay. The winery also acquires grapes from other sources. One is the prestigious Three Palms Vineyard just southeast of the winery and owned by Sloan Upton, Sterling's first vineyard manager, and his brother John.

When the winery was established, the owners were confident about the future of Cabernet Sauvignon, but took a chance on three then-unproven varietals—Sauvignon Blanc, Chardonnay, and Merlot—by including them in early vineyard plantings. Consequently, in 1969, Sterling Vineyards became the first American producer of a vintage-dated Napa Valley Merlot.

STERLING VINEYARDS
1111 Dunaweal Ln.
Calistoga, CA 94515
707-942-3344
800-726-6136
info@sterlingvineyards.com
www.sterlingvineyards.com

OWNER: Diageo Chateau & Estate Wines.

LOCATION: Just south of Calistoga between Hwy. 29 and Silverado Trail.

APPELLATION: Napa Valley.

HOURS: 10:30 A.M.–4:30 P.M. daily.

TASTINGS: $15 for 5 wines ($20, weekends and holidays, April–October), $45 for Reserve Tasting.

TOURS: Self-guided during operating hours. Groups by appointment.

THE WINES: Cabernet Sauvignon, Chardonnay, Malvasia Bianca, Merlot, Muscat Canelli, Pinot Gris, Pinot Noir, Sangiovese, Sauvignon Blanc, Syrah, Viognier, Zinfandel.

SPECIALTIES: Vineyard-designated Cabernet Sauvignon, Chardonnay, Merlot, and Pinot Noir; reserve Cabernet Sauvignon, Chardonnay, and Merlot.

WINEMAKERS: Mike Westrick and Chris Millard.

ANNUAL PRODUCTION: 400,000 cases.

OF SPECIAL NOTE: Children are given juice, crayons, and notecards to color. Annual events include Merlot in May. Historic collection of wine art and artifacts. Ten wines made for Cellar Club members available to general public only at winery.

NEARBY ATTRACTIONS: Bothe-Napa State Park; Robert Louis Stevenson State Park; Old Faithful Geyser of California; Petrified Forest; Sharpsteen Museum (exhibits on Robert Louis Stevenson and Walt Disney animator Ben Sharpsteen).

SWANSON VINEYARDS AND WINERY

**SWANSON VINEYARDS
AND WINERY**
1271 Manley Ln.
Rutherford, CA 94573
707-967-3500
salon@swansonvineyards.
com
www.swansonvineyards.
com

OWNER:
W. Clarke Swanson, Jr.

LOCATION: .5 mile west of
Hwy. 29.

APPELLATION: Napa Valley.

HOURS: By appointment
Wednesday–Sunday,
11 A.M., 1:30 P.M., and 4 P.M.

TASTINGS: Choice of
tailored tastings, $25
and $55.

TOURS: None.

THE WINES: Alexis
(Cabernet Sauvignon
blend), Angelica, Merlot,
Petite Sirah, Pinot Grigio,
Rosato, Sangiovese,
late-harvest Semillon,
Sparkling Muscat, Syrah.

SPECIALTIES: Alexis, Merlot.

WINEMAKER: Chris Phelps.

ANNUAL PRODUCTION:
25,000 cases.

OF SPECIAL NOTE: Tastings
include food pairings.
Number of guests limited
to 8. Angelica, Muscat,
Syrah, Rosato, Sangiovese,
Late-Harvest Semillon,
and Petite Sirah available
only at winery.

NEARBY ATTRACTIONS:
Silverado Museum
(Robert Louis Stevenson
memorabilia); Napa Valley
Museum (winemaking
displays, art exhibits).

Time seems to stand still when you step inside the Swanson Salon. Or maybe the Salon takes you back to an earlier era of leisure, luxury, and lingering conversation. For one hour at least, visitors can forget the outside world and concentrate on the wine and their fellow tasters. Only eight people are seated at each tasting session. Surrounded by fine things and served one wine after another, visitors are guided by the "salonnier" through that day's menu of wines, accompanied by little plates of elegant cheeses and American caviar atop potato chips, and capped with a bonbon made exclusively for Swanson, paired with the final wine.

At the appointed hour, arriving into the stucco winery with its fantasy begins when they step into an with coral-colored walls adorned by tall as eight feet, by noted Bay Area they make up his *Vintage Peasant* created especially for this room. Then table made of Moroccan wood inlaid day's offerings, which are already them are wines available only at the winery.

visitors are welcomed by the host weathered blue window shutters. The intimate, intensely decorated room seventeen colorful paintings, some as figurative artist Ira Yeager. Together, series, most of the works having been it is time to take a seat at an octagonal with agate. A small menu lists the arranged on the table. Always among

According to Alexis Swanson, director of marketing, the salon concept coalesced in 2000 as an expression of the Swanson family's affinity for an old-fashioned way of life. "It's all about service and intimacy and obsessive attention to detail," she says. "Every tasting is like a little cocktail party held in each guest's honor. The common thread is a love of wine, but the conversation is never technical. It's all a balance of humor and whimsy, art and theater." One look around the jewel box of a room proves Swanson's point. Details of the decor may change slightly over the years, but the style, established by noted New York interior designer Tom Britt, does not.

Catering to the traveler looking for the less attainable, the Salon offers such small-batch wines as Angelica, Rosato, Sangiovese, Syrah, late-harvest Semillon, Petite Sirah, and a sparkling Muscat—wines found only at the Swanson Salon.

TWOMEY CELLARS

One of the very few wineries devoted to *soutirage traditional* winemaking, Twomey Cellars produces primarily Merlot. All of the grapes for the Merlot come from a single Napa Valley vineyard, the Soda Canyon Ranch. The focus on Merlot allows the winemaker to practice painstaking, time-honored techniques that maximize the inherent qualities of the grapes.

Twomey (pronounced "TOO-mee") Cellars opened the winery and tasting room in June 2003. Both are located in the northern part of Napa Valley, just south of Calistoga on Highway 29. The sleek, but intimate, tasting room is housed in 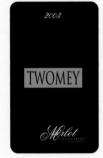 one of two matching clapboard cottages in front of the winemaking facility. The gleaming white buildings are surrounded by landscaped gardens and flourishing vineyards.

But it is the grapevines in the southeastern Napa Valley that provide the fruit for Twomey Cellars Merlot. The 145-acre Soda Canyon Ranch sits on deep volcanic soil and is tightly planted with French Merlot vines selected for their low yield of small, intensely flavored berries. The long, warm days in this area are perfect for ripening sugar levels, while the cool, foggy breezes from nearby San Pablo Bay extend the growing season without the risk of overripening the fruit.

Soda Canyon Ranch produces a particularly complex Merlot that warrants meticulous handling. Twomey winemaker Daniel Baron became well versed in the *soutirage traditional* approach used in Bordeaux when he spent a year working in Pomerol and St. Emilion. Few other California wineries apply this French technique to Merlot. Essentially, it is a slow, careful process whereby the wine is decanted from one barrel to another without the disruptive effects of a pump. This method, refined over centuries, remains the ideal way to clarify red wines to crystal-clear brilliance while drawing the fruit characteristics forward and softening the tannins.

The grapes are crushed and their juice fermented before being moved into thin-staved French oak barrels. During eighteen months of aging, the wine is racked five times, a process that removes the wine from the lees, or solid sediments, which fall to the bottom of the barrel. Each barrel has two reed-wrapped stoppers, called *esquives,* in its head. Following the *soutirage traditional* method, the cellar worker removes an *esquive* and replaces it with a bronze valve that allows the wine to flow by gravity or air pressure until he sees the first sign of sediment. He then stops the flow, leaving behind a small amount of cloudy wine. The clear wine is transferred into a second barrel, a method that preserves its full aromatic intensity and fosters a smooth, silky texture.

TWOMEY CELLARS
1183 Dunaweal Ln.
Calistoga, CA 94515
800-505-4850
www.twomeycellars.com

OWNERS:
Duncan family.

LOCATION: 2 miles south of Calistoga at corner of Hwy. 29.

APPELLATION: Napa Valley.

HOURS: 9 A.M.–4 P.M. Monday–Saturday.

TASTING: $5 (includes complimentary wineglass).

TOURS: Monday–Friday, reservations recommended. Saturday by appointment.

THE WINE: Merlot.

SPECIALTY: Merlot.

WINEMAKER:
Daniel H. Baron.

ANNUAL PRODUCTION:
10,000 cases.

OF SPECIAL NOTE: The latest vintage is released each year in October and is available in limited quantity.

NEARBY ATTRACTIONS:
Bothe-Napa State Park (hiking, picnicking, horseback riding, swimming Memorial Day–Labor Day); Robert Louis Stevenson State Park (hiking); hot-air balloon rides; Old Faithful Geyser of California; Petrified Forest; Sharpsteen Museum (exhibits on Robert Louis Stevenson and Walt Disney animator Ben Sharpsteen).

VINE CLIFF WINERY

VINE CLIFF WINERY
7400 Silverado Trail
Napa, CA 94558
707-944-1364
info@vinecliff.com
www.vinecliff.com

OWNERS: Sweeney family.

LOCATION: On Silverado Trail less than .5 miles south of Oakville Cross Rd.

APPELLATION: Oakville.

HOURS: By appointment, 10 A.M.–4:30 P.M. daily.

TASTINGS: $20 for 3 or more wines.

TOURS: Daily, by appointment.

THE WINES: Cabernet Sauvignon, Chardonnay, Merlot.

SPECIALTIES: "Private Stock" Cabernet Sauvignon, Proprietress Reserve Chardonnay.

WINEMAKER: Rex Smith.

ANNUAL PRODUCTION: 8,000 cases.

OF SPECIAL NOTE: Tours visit winery's 15,000-square-foot barrel-aging cave. "Private Stock" Cabernet Sauvignon and Proprietress Reserve Chardonnay available only at winery.

NEARBY ATTRACTIONS: Napa Valley Museum (winemaking displays, art exhibits).

Nestled into a hidden canyon in the prestigious Oakville Appellation, Vine Cliff Winery boasts one of the most desirable locations in the Napa Valley. The surrounding hillsides above the Silverado Trail are home to the stunning vineyards that produce the grapes for rich, full-bodied Cabernet Sauvignons.

This peaceful, ultra-private enclave was once part of the sprawling estate owned by pioneer grape grower George Yount. More than 130 years ago, George Burrage and Thomas Tucker recognized its potential as a great winery location and bought the property. The farsighted entrepreneurs removed hundreds of tons of rocks from the slopes and gradually transformed them into a thriving expanse of vineyards. They constructed a winery four stories high and carved tunnels beneath the vineyards where they aged their wines  in the best conditions. The partners called their new enterprise Vine Cliff Winery. Their vision was carried on by John Fry, the wealthy San Franciscan who bought the property in the 1880s and quickly established Vine Cliff as a premier gathering spot for leaders of the agri- cultural, business, and social worlds of nineteenth-century Napa Valley and San Francisco. Fry began planting trees and formal gardens, laying the groundwork for the extensive landscaping that continues to imbue the winery with grace and charm. Intriguingly, Vine Cliff is among a handful of early Napa Valley wine estates—now known as "ghost wineries"—that were inexplicably abandoned in the 1890s.

Nearly a century later, Charles and Nell Sweeney purchased the estate and set out to restore Vine Cliff to its former glory. Their son, Rob Sweeney, spent long hours on horseback to familiarize himself with the terrain, which is now terraced and planted with twenty-one acres of Cabernet Sauvignon. The Sweeney family's respect for the land is evidenced by their commitment to the principles of sustainable viticulture. They employ organic practices like enriching the soil through techniques such as planting native species of grasses as a ground cover between the rows of vines and allowing them to compost naturally. Over the past decade, a most ecologically complex and diverse biosystem has been established at Vine Cliff estate vineyards, resulting in the protection of its wildlife and habitat.

Winemaker Rex Smith, who was raised on a farm in New Zealand, believes that the best wines are made from fruit that expresses the vineyard. Vine Cliff Winery prides itself on small lots of intensely flavored handmade wines—including Cabernet Sauvignons as well as bold Chardonnays from the acclaimed Carneros District.

ZD WINES

Driving along the Silverado Trail through the heart of the Napa Valley, travelers are sure to notice the entrance to ZD Wines. A two-ton boulder, extracted from one of ZD's mountain vineyards, is adorned by the winery's striking gold logo, beckoning them to stop for a visit. Calla lilies intertwined with lavender welcome guests as they stroll along the path and underneath an intimate arbor to the winery entrance. The tasting room provides a cool respite on a hot summer day or a warm and cozy place to linger in front of a fireplace in the winter. Behind the tasting bar, shaped like a large barrel, are windows that allow visitors to peer into ZD's aging cellars as they sample ZD Chardonnay, Pinot Noir, and Cabernet Sauvignon.

It has been said that winemaking isn't rocket science, but in fact, founding partner Norman deLeuze had been designing liquid rocket engines for Aerojet-General in Sacramento when he met his original partner Gino Zepponi. They decided to collaborate on producing classic Pinot Noir and Chardonnay varietals and needed a name for their new enterprise. The aeronautical industry had a quality-control program with the initials ZD, referring to Zero Defects. This matched the partners' initials and created a new association for the letters ZD. In 1969, the winery purchased Pinot Noir grapes from the Winery Lake Vineyard in Carneros in southern Sonoma and produced its first wine, the first ever labeled with the Carneros appellation. Soon after, the winery started making Chardonnay, which continues to be ZD's flagship wine.

Norman deLeuze turned to winemaking full-time, while his wife, Rosa Lee, handled sales and marketing. They purchased six acres, built their own winery, and planted Cabernet Sauvignon in Rutherford in 1979. Four years later, son Robert deLeuze was named winemaker. He had been working in ZD's cellars since he was twelve and later studied at the University of California at Davis. In 2001, Robert passed the winemaking reins to Chris Pisani, who had worked closely with Robert for five years, building his appreciation and understanding of the family's consistent winemaking style.

As ZD enters its thirty-seventh year of winemaking, it is still owned and operated by Norman, Rosa Lee, and their three adult children: Robert as wine master and CEO, Brett as president, and Julie as administrative director. Robert's two children, Brandon and Jill, began working summers and holidays at ZD in their early teens, bringing a third generation to this family affair.

ZD WINES
8383 Silverado Trail
Napa, CA 94558
800-487-7757
info@zdwines.com
www.zdwines.com

OWNERS: deLeuze family.

LOCATION: About 2.5 miles south of Zinfandel Ln.

APPELLATION: Rutherford.

HOURS: 10 A.M.–4:30 P.M. daily.

TASTINGS: $10 for 3 or 4 current releases; $15 for 2 or 3 reserve or older vintage wines.

TOURS: By appointment ($5).

THE WINES: Abacus (solera-style blend of ZD Reserve Cabernet Sauvignon), Cabernet Sauvignon, Chardonnay, Pinot Noir.

SPECIALTIES: Cabernet Sauvignon, Chardonnay, Pinot Noir.

WINEMAKERS: Robert deLeuze, wine master; Chris Pisani, winemaker.

ANNUAL PRODUCTION: 30,000 cases.

OF SPECIAL NOTE: Sit-down wine and cheese seminars on Saturdays at 11 A.M. by appointment ($25, 12-person limit). Sensory Component tastings on Sundays at 11 A.M. by appointment ($25, 12-person limit).

NEARBY ATTRACTIONS: Bothe-Napa State Park (hiking, picnicking, horseback riding, swimming Memorial Day–Labor Day); Bale Grist Mill State Historic Park (waterpowered mill circa 1846); Silverado Museum (Robert Louis Stevenson memorabilia).

SONOMA

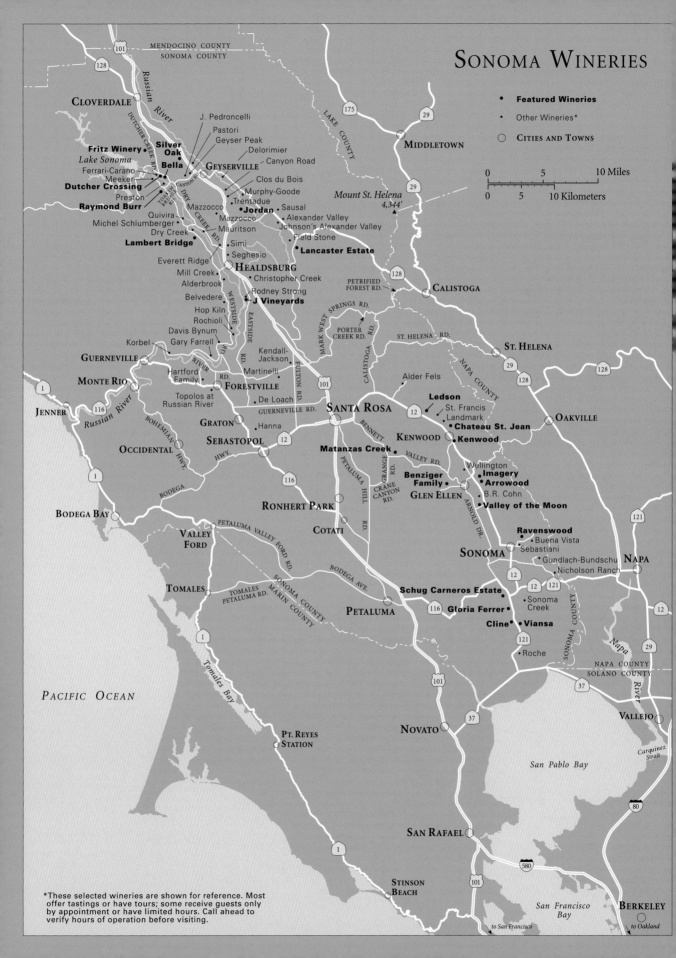

Sonoma boasts the greatest geographical diversity and the highest number of appellations in California wine country. From the Pacific Coast to the inland valleys, to the Mayacamas Range that defines the eastern border with Napa County, the countryside is crisscrossed by dozens of rural roads, making it an ideal destination for casual exploration.

Most of the county's oldest wineries can be found in the historic town of Sonoma. Facing the eight-acre central plaza are nineteenth-century adobe and false-front buildings that now house shops, restaurants,  inns, and historic sites. Diverse luminaries, such as the horticulturist Luther Burbank and the cartoonist Charles Schulz of "Peanuts" fame, made their homes in Santa Rosa; no trip would be complete without visiting the museums named for them. North of Santa Rosa, the Russian River wends its way to the coast, offering boating, swimming, and fishing opportunities and the shade of giant redwoods along its banks.

Healdsburg, which has quickly evolved from a quiet backwater into the hottest destination in the county, is at the hub of three major grape-growing regions—Russian River Valley, Alexander Valley, and Dry Creek Valley—all within a ten-minute drive of the vibrant town plaza.

ARROWOOD VINEYARDS & WINERY

**ARROWOOD VINEYARDS
& WINERY**
14347 Hwy. 12
Glen Ellen, CA 95442
707-935-2600
hospitality@
arrowoodvineyards.com
www.arrowoodvineyards.
com

FOUNDERS: Richard and
Alis Arrowood.

LOCATION: About 3 miles
north of town of Sonoma
via Hwy 12.

APPELLATION:
Sonoma Valley.

HOURS: 10 A.M.–4:30 P.M.
daily.

TASTINGS: $5 for 4 wines;
$10 for 4 reserve wines.

TOURS: 10:30 A.M. and
2:30 P.M. daily by
appointment.

THE WINES: Cabernet
Sauvignon, Chardonnay,
Gewürztraminer, Malbec,
Merlot, Pinot Blanc, red
Rhône blend, white Rhône
blend, Riesling (late har-
vest), Syrah, Viognier.

SPECIALTY: All wines are
made from Sonoma
County grapes.

WINEMAKER:
Richard Arrowood.

ANNUAL PRODUCTION:
30,000 cases.

OF SPECIAL NOTE: Extended
winery and cellar tours
by appointment; various
events ranging from
barrel-making demonstra-
tions to food-and-wine
pairings. Wine accessories,
gifts, and apparel sold at
winery shop.

NEARBY ATTRACTIONS:
Jack London State Historic
Park (museum, hiking,
horseback riding); Sonoma
Valley Regional Park
(hiking, dog park).

From the highway, the pair of gray, New England farmhouse-style buildings with generous porches neatly trimmed in white could easily pass for a country inn. In fact, the property was originally intended to become a bed-and-breakfast, but it never opened for business. Today, these handsome, sedate structures are home to the Arrowood Winery. The sweeping view from the wide porches encompasses the Arrowood vineyards, a neighboring winery, and the oak-studded slopes of Sonoma Mountain on the western horizon.

Richard Arrowood made his name as the longtime winemaker at Chateau St. Jean, just up the road in Kenwood. A native  San Franciscan raised in Santa Rosa, he earned degrees in organic chemistry and enology, and got his start in the business in 1965 at Korbel Champagne Cellars. In 1974 the founders of Chateau St. Jean hired Arrowood as their first employee. For the next sixteen years, he made wines that earned both him and the winery worldwide attention. His reputation as one of the country's best winemakers was firmly established with his late-harvest Riesling, a varietal that he produces today under his own label.

In the late 1980s, he met and married Alis Demers, who had been working in the wine industry since 1978. Together, they began establishing the Arrowood brand. They found the perfect ten-acre property and designed their winery to blend harmoniously with the rural landscape. When they realized that they had inherited two donkeys, Burt and Ernie, from the previous landowner, they lacked the heart to kick them out and fenced off an area behind the winery.

While Richard was still at Chateau St. Jean, Alis was topping barrels or running the bottling line when she wasn't giving tours and conducting tastings. Richard began working full-time at the winery in 1990, freeing Alis to devote her energies to sales and marketing. Richard began by focusing exclusively on reserve-quality Chardonnay and Cabernet Sauvignon. Before long, he was seduced by the idea of working with less common varietals, particularly when he found exceptional fruit. Today Arrowood produces Malbec, for instance, as well as more familiar wines, all made from Sonoma County grapes.

In 1998 the winery realized a long-cherished dream: opening a spacious Hospitality House next door. The building has a dramatic vaulted ceiling, an enormous stone fireplace flanked by comfortable seating, and a second-floor loft for private events. Picture windows afford magnificent views of Sonoma Valley. Visitors are welcome to walk out the huge glass doors and relax on the wraparound veranda, wineglasses in hand.

BELLA VINEYARDS AND WINE CAVES

Located on the banks of Dry Creek, this rustic winery has a fairy-tale quality. The refurbished, red-sided barn, the ancient olive trees with their giant, gnarled trunks, and the vineyards thriving above the cave entrance could be an illustration right out of an old-fashioned children's book.

The tale is a romantic one with a happy-ever-after ending. In 1994 Lynn and Scott Adams came to the Sonoma wine country to get married and fell in love all over again—with the land. They made another vow: to devote themselves to living in a rural setting and to making fine red wine. After all, the Dry Creek Valley has long been famous for its abundance of very old Zinfandel vines known

for producing small amounts of highly flavored grapes. A year later, the young couple bought their first Zinfandel vineyard, on ninety-three acres at the western end of the valley. Before long, Lynn and Scott had moved to the area to manage the property. They spent several years taking viticulture classes at the University of California, Davis, and elsewhere before they felt ready to make wine. By the time they opened the winery, they knew exactly what to call the place. Bella is named in honor of their two daughters, who arrived around the same time as their first wine barrels.

To realize the other part of their dream—making fine red wine— the Adamses purchased two more low-yielding vineyards not far from their original property. The grapes for Bella's Grenache and estate Zinfandel come from eighty-five-year-old vines at Lily Hill Estate, as the original property is called. Bella also harvests Zinfandel from the Belle Canyon Vineyard on the east side of Dry Creek Valley, where old-clone, low-yielding vines deliver intensely flavored grapes. The third family vineyard, the Big River Ranch on the border of the Russian River and Alexander Valley appellations, is a veritable forest of hundred-year-old Zinfandel, Syrah, and Petite Sirah vines. Bella Vineyards does not need huge crops to make its wines—in fact, quite the opposite. The first vintage, 1999, consisted of only 200 cases. By focusing on single-vineyard wines and limiting production to a maximum of 7,500 cases, the Adamses have the option of postponing release dates until the wine is sufficiently aged and completely ready to drink.

As a family winery located in a quiet residential neighborhood, Bella is appropriately low-key. Tastings are conducted inside the high-ceilinged aging caves, which are furnished with bistro tables and decorated with antique winery artifacts from around the world. The grounds are a popular destination for picnickers and amateur landscape artists, who, like Lynn and Scott Adams, find inspiration in the views of vineyards and rolling hills.

BELLA VINEYARDS AND WINE CAVES
9711 West Dry Creek Rd.
Healdsburg, CA 95448
707-473-9171
866-572-3552
info@bellawinery.com
www.bellawinery.com

OWNERS: Scott and Lynn Adams.

LOCATION: 9 miles northwest of Healdsburg via Dry Creek Rd. and Yoakim Bridge Rd.

APPELLATION: Dry Creek Valley.

HOURS: 11 A.M.–4:30 P.M. daily.

TASTINGS: Complimentary.

TOURS: Group tours by appointment.

THE WINES: Petit Sirah, Syrah, Zinfandel.

SPECIALTIES: Vineyard-designated Syrah and Zinfandel.

WINEMAKER: Joe Healy.

ANNUAL PRODUCTION: 5,000 cases.

OF SPECIAL NOTE: Tasting room is in a 6,700-square-foot cave. Picnic area is partially shaded by 100-year-old olive trees. Limits on the purchase of specialty production wines. Annual events include Winter Wineland (January), Barrel Tasting (March), Passport to Dry Creek Valley (April), Wine & Food Affair (November).

NEARBY ATTRACTIONS: Lake Sonoma (hiking, fishing, boating).

BENZIGER FAMILY WINERY

BENZIGER FAMILY WINERY
1883 London Ranch Rd.
Glen Ellen, CA 95442
888-490-2739
greatwine@benziger.com
www.benziger.com

OWNERS: Benziger family.

LOCATION: About .5 mile from Arnold Dr.

APPELLATION: Sonoma Mountain.

HOURS: 10 A.M.–5 P.M. Monday–Friday.

TASTINGS: $5 for 5 wines; $10 for 5 reserve wines.

TOURS: $10 for tram tour and 4 tastings.

THE WINES: Cabernet Sauvignon, Chardonnay, Merlot, Muscat, Pinot Noir, Sauvignon Blanc, Syrah.

SPECIALTIES: Bordeaux blends, biodynamic wines.

WINEMAKERS: Mike and Joe Benziger.

ANNUAL PRODUCTION: 200,000 cases.

OF SPECIAL NOTE: Picnic area in redwood grove; children's play area; peacock aviary; display of antique farm and winery equipment; shop with home furnishings and cookbooks. Vineyard-designated and estate wines available only at winery. Annual events include Barrel Tasting (March), Pinot Passion (February).

NEARBY ATTRACTIONS: Jack London State Historic Park (museum, hiking, horseback riding); Sonoma Valley Regional Park (hiking, dog park); Morton's Sonoma Springs Resort (swimming, picnicking in summer).

The Benziger family's pride and joy is the snazzy red Massey 375 tractor that takes visitors on forty-five-minute tram tours of the winery's estate vineyards and gardens. Part of the fun is scouting for the songbirds, butterflies, and small animals that populate the estate's three wildlife sanctuaries, along with a host of beneficial insects that provide a natural form of pest control. By encouraging the public to get up close and personal with their eighty-five-acre ranch, the Benzigers share their love of the land and show visitors how they use organic farming practices to cultivate grapes that reflect the specific attributes of the each vineyard block.

More than twenty-five years ago, Mike and Mary Benziger drove a short distance up Sonoma Mountain from the hamlet of Glen Ellen. There, abutting author Jack London's historic Beauty Ranch, they found the overgrown property that, with the help of Mike's parents, Bruno and Helen Benziger, would become the Benziger Family Winery. The couple were soon joined by Mike's six siblings and their parents. Today, more than two dozen members of the clan live on and around the estate.

Benziger Family Winery occupies a 360-degree bowl formed by volcanic explosions from Sonoma Mountain some two million years ago that created a wide spectrum of sun exposures, elevations, and soil profiles. The Benzigers found that the Sonoma Valley's warm-to-hot days and cool nights are well suited to several grape varieties, particularly Cabernet Sauvignon, which is planted in 65 percent of the estate vineyards.

United not only by blood but also by a commitment to sustainable agriculture, the Benzigers adhere to the highest form of organic farming. Biodynamics requires the elimination of all chemicals and artificial inputs in order to encourage the most natural and healthy environment in and around the vineyards. In 2000 the Benziger property became the first vineyard in either Napa or Sonoma County to be certified biodynamic by the Demeter Association, the only group with that authority. The highest expression of Benziger's winegrowing practices is Tribute, a red Bordeaux blend produced from 100 percent estate grapes that debuted with the 2001 vintage. The winery encourages biodynamic practices among its fifty growers. In all, Benziger has access to some three hundred separate vineyard lots that provide enough variety to warrant bottling more than twenty different wines a year. Visitors do not have to take the tractor-tram tour to sample some of these wines in the tasting room, but it would be a shame to miss the best adventure ride in the wine country.

CHATEAU ST. JEAN WINERY

With the dramatic profile of Sugarloaf Ridge as a backdrop, the exquisitely landscaped grounds at Chateau St. Jean in Kenwood evoke the image of a grand country estate. The chateau itself dates to the 1920s, but it wasn't until 1973 that a family of Central Valley, California, growers of table grapes founded the winery. They named it after a favorite relative and, with tongue in cheek, placed a statue of "St. Jean" in the garden.

The winery building was constructed from the ground up to suit Chateau St. Jean's particular style of winemaking. The founders believed in the European practice of creating vineyard-designated wines, so  they designed the winery to accommodate numerous lots of grapes, which could be kept separate throughout the winemaking process. Wines from each special vineyard are also bottled and marketed separately, with the vineyard name on the label. The winery produces eleven vineyard-designated wines from the Sonoma Valley, Alexander Valley, Russian River Valley, and Carneros appellations. The winery also makes other premium varietals and one famously successful blend.

Chateau St. Jean became the first Sonoma winery to be awarded the prestigious Wine of the Year award from *Wine Spectator* magazine for its 1996 Cinq Cépages, a Bordeaux-style blend of five varieties. The winery received high aclaim again when it was given the #2 Wine of the Year from *Wine Spectator* for its 1999 Cinq Cépages Cabernet Sauvignon. Winemaker Margo Van Staaveren has more than twenty years of vineyard and winemaking experience with Chateau St. Jean, and her knowledge of Sonoma further underscores her excellence in highlighting the best of each vineyard.

In the summer of 2000, Chateau St. Jean opened the doors to its new Visitor Center and Gardens. A formal Mediterranean-style garden contains roses, herbs, and citrus trees planted in oversized terra-cotta urns arranged to create a number of open-air "rooms." Picnickers have always been welcome to relax on the winery's redwood-studded grounds, but now the setting is enhanced by the extensive plantings, making the one-acre garden attractive throughout the year.

Beyond the Mediterranean garden is the tasting room with a custom-made tasting bar. Fashioned from mahogany with ebony accents, the thirty-five-foot-long bar is topped with sheet zinc. The elegant chateau houses the Reserve Tasting Room. Visitors who would like to learn more about Chateau St. Jean wines are encouraged to attend the winery's educational seminars on food-and-wine pairing and other subjects. Introductory classes are offered daily, while more in-depth programs are available by reservation.

CHATEAU ST. JEAN WINERY
8555 Hwy. 12
Kenwood, CA 95452
707-833-4134
www.chateaustjean.com

OWNER: Foster's Wine Estates Americas.

LOCATION: 8 miles east of Santa Rosa off U.S. 101.

APPELLATION: Sonoma Valley.

HOURS: 10 A.M.–5 P.M. daily.

TASTINGS: $5 for 3 wines in Tasting Room; $10 in Reserve Tasting Room.

TOURS: By appointment.

THE WINES: Cabernet Franc, Cabernet Sauvignon, Chardonnay, Fumé Blanc, Gewürtztraminer, Late-Harvest Johannisberg Riesling, Merlot, Pinot Blanc, Pinot Noir, Riesling, Viognier.

SPECIALTY: Vineyard-designated wines.

WINEMAKER: Margo Van Staaveren.

ANNUAL PRODUCTION: 300,000 cases.

OF SPECIAL NOTE: Picnic tables in oak-and-redwood grove. Classes and seminars on wine. Open houses on most holidays. Large store offering local cheeses, meats, and breads, as well as other merchandise.

NEARBY ATTRACTIONS: Sugarloaf Ridge State Park (hiking, camping, horseback riding).

CLINE CELLARS

CLINE CELLARS
24737 Hwy. 121
Sonoma, CA 95476
707-940-4000
800-546-2070
info@clinecellars.com
www.clinecellars.com

OWNERS:
Fred and Nancy Cline.

LOCATION: About 5 miles
south of the town of
Sonoma.

APPELLATION: Los Carneros.

HOURS: 10 A.M.–6 P.M. daily.

TASTINGS: Complimentary.

TOURS: 11 A.M., 1 P.M., and
3 P.M. daily.

THE WINES: Carignane,
Marsanne, Mourvèdre,
Pinot Grigio, Syrah,
Viognier, Zinfandel.

SPECIALTIES: Zinfandel,
Rhône-style wines.

WINEMAKER:
Charles Tsegeletos.

ANNUAL PRODUCTION:
200,000 cases.

OF SPECIAL NOTE: Free
museum displaying
handcrafted models of
California's Spanish mis-
sions, originally created
for the 1939 World's Fair.
Aviaries with exotic birds.
Cookbooks, deli items,
condiments, and gifts sold
in winery shop.

NEARBY ATTRACTIONS:
Mission San Francisco
Solano and other historic
buildings in downtown
Sonoma; Infineon Raceway
(NASCAR and other
events); biplane flights;
Cornerstone Festival of
Gardens (high-concept
landscape installations);
Viansa Winery Wetlands
(tours).

Five thousand rosebushes stand shoulder to shoulder beside the low stone wall that winds its way onto the winery grounds. From April through December, they provide a riot of fragrant pink, white, red, peach, lavender, and yellow blossoms. Picnic tables are scattered around the lawn, shaded by magnolias and other trees. Weeping willows hover over the mineral pools on either side of the restored 1850s farmhouse where the tasting room is located. The white farmhouse is rimmed with a picturesque dark green porch set with small wrought-iron tables and chairs where visitors can sip wine at their leisure.

Cline Cellars was originally established in Oakley, California, some forty miles east of San Francisco. Founder Fred Cline learning farming and winemaking Jacuzzi (of spa and pump fame). with a $12,000 inheritance from later, his brother Matt joined Cline studying viticulture at the University Cline Cellars facilities were relocated Carneros District at the southern had spent his childhood summers from his grandfather, Valeriano Cline started the winery in 1982 the sale of Jacuzzi Bros. Four years Cellars as the winemaker after of California at Davis. In 1991, the to this 350-acre estate in the end of the Sonoma Valley.

The Cline estate occupies a historical parcel of land first settled by the Miwok Indians. Nearby, a nineteenth-century bathhouse harks to the time when the white settlers realized something that the Miwoks had known all along: warm mineral baths are good for you. While the town of Sonoma is generally considered the original site of the Sonoma mission, the mission was actually founded here when Father Altimira installed a cross on July 4, 1823. Perhaps it was the constant Carneros breezes that inspired him to pull up stakes and relocate to the town of Sonoma later that same year.

Cline specializes in Zinfandel and Rhône varietals. Their Ancient Vines Carignane, Zinfandel, and Mourvèdre wines are produced from some of the oldest and rarest vines in the state. The Mourvèdre grapevines represent approximately 85 percent of California's total supply of this versatile varietal. The Sonoma location was selected especially for its relatively cool climate; chilly fog and frequent strong afternoon winds mitigate the summertime heat that blisters the rest of the Sonoma Valley. When the Clines bought the property, they planted all-new vineyards of Rhône varietals such as Syrah, Viognier, Marsanne, and Roussanne.

DUTCHER CROSSING

Bigger is not necessarily better. That's the philosophy behind this boutique operation, which released its first commercial wines—fewer than three thousand cases—in 2005. When the winery reaches its target capacity, probably in 2011, it will produce a maximum of only nine thousand cases.

Dutcher Crossing founders Bruce Nevins and Jim Stevens are not short on ambition. For them, it's all about quality, not quantity. By limiting production, Dutcher Crossing can continue to focus on small, mostly single-vineyard lots. Although about half the grapes come from other sources in the Dry Creek, Russian River, and Alexander valleys, the estate vineyard accounts for the remainder, allowing the winery to concentrate on the best Dry Creek has to offer.

A sense of place is at the heart of Dutcher Crossing. Surrounded on all sides by vineyards, the winery was designed to resemble an early 1900s Dry Creek Valley barn, complete with cupolas and a pitched roof. The cedar building is split by a large breezeway that serves as a picture frame, affording a panoramic view of the vineyards and hillsides across the creek. This is the setting that convinced Bruce Nevins, who has lived in the nearby Alexander Valley since the early 1990s, and his friend Jim Stevens to start a winery in Dry Creek Valley in 2001. The pair have been doing business together since they cofounded Perrier North America and helped spearhead the bottled water craze in the United States some thirty years ago, before going on to market and distribute several domestic and international wine brands.

The tasting room, located across the breezeway from the production and storage facilities, has wide hickory plank floors, a polished limestone tasting bar, a vaulted beam ceiling, and tall windows on two sides. At one end, a cozy conversational area has deeply cushioned wingback chairs surrounding a low, round, century-old pine table set on an antique braided rug. The fireplace mantel was fashioned from distressed railroad ties; the hearth consists of locally quarried stone. Above it hangs an abstract painting of the Dry Creek Valley by noted regional artist Wade Hoefer. A collection of vintage baskets completes the impression of an old American farmstead.

At Dutcher Crossing, the emphasis is on soaking up this picturesque appellation, where most of the wineries are small and family owned. Throughout Dry Creek Valley, the ambience is casual and the pace, relaxed. Visitors are encouraged to linger as long as they like. They can buy artisanal fare in the tasting room and enjoy an alfresco luncheon in a trellised picnic area. With the vineyards in the foreground and Bradford Mountain as a backdrop, the pristinely pastoral view is mesmerizing.

DUTCHER CROSSING
8533 Dry Creek Rd.
Healdsburg, CA 95448
707-431-2700
866-431-2711
info@dutchercrossing
winery.com
www.dutchercrossing
winery.com

OWNERS: Bruce Nevins and Jim Stevens.

LOCATION: 9 miles northwest of Healdsburg via Dry Creek Rd.

APPELLATION: Dry Creek Valley.

HOURS: 11 A.M.–5 P.M. daily.

TASTINGS: $5 for 6 or 7 wines (applicable to wine purchase).

TOURS: Private tour and tasting with owners by appointment.

THE WINES: Cabernet Sauvignon, Chardonnay, Sauvignon Blanc, Zinfandel.

SPECIALTY: Cabernet Sauvignon–Syrah blends.

WINEMAKER: Kerry Damskey.

ANNUAL PRODUCTION: 4,000 cases.

OF SPECIAL NOTE: Covered patio for picnickers. Regional artisanal cheeses, meats, breads, and olive oil sold in tasting room. Annual events include Winter Wineland (January), Barrel Tasting (March), Passport to Dry Creek Valley (April), Wine & Food Affair (November).

NEARBY ATTRACTIONS: Lake Sonoma (boating, camping, hiking).

FRITZ WINERY

FRITZ WINERY
24691 Dutcher Creek Rd.
Cloverdale, CA 95425
707-894-3389
800-418-9463
info@fritzwinery.com
www.fritzwinery.com

PRESIDENT:
Clayton B. Fritz.

LOCATION: About 1 mile
southwest of intersection
of U.S. 101 and Dutcher
Creek Rd.

APPELLATION:
Dry Creek Valley.

HOURS: 10:30 A.M.–4:30 P.M.
daily.

TASTINGS: Complimentary
for all wines.

TOURS: By appointment.

THE WINES: Cabernet
Sauvignon, Chardonnay,
Estate Zinfandel, Late-
Harvest Zinfandel, Pinot
Noir, Sauvignon Blanc,
Syrah, Zin Rosé, Zinfandel.

SPECIALTIES: Cabernet,
Chardonnay, Pinot Noir.

WINEMAKER:
Christina Pallmann.

ANNUAL PRODUCTION:
18,000 cases.

OF SPECIAL NOTE:
Annual events include
Winter Wineland
(January), Barrel Tasting
(March), Dry Creek
Passport Weekend (April).
Late-harvest Zinfandel,
Ruxton Chardonnay, and
Syrah available only
at winery.

NEARBY ATTRACTIONS:
Russian River (swimming,
canoe and kayak rentals);
Lake Sonoma (boating,
camping, hiking).

What began as an idyllic family retreat is now a thriving family business on the northern edge of the Dry Creek Valley. Jay and Barbara Fritz were seeking an escape from the summertime fog and bustle of San Francisco when they found this rugged, hundred-plus-acre property on a remote hillside back in 1970. They dammed a spring to create "Lake Fritz" and created a home away from home. Son Clayton Fritz spent his childhood summers there, although it has been a long time since he swam in the pond. Now, as president of the winery built in 1979—still the northernmost facility in Sonoma County—and as the only one of the three siblings to work there, he is far too busy looking after day-to-day operations.

Construction of the winery began when energy crises were commonplace. The idea of an energy-efficient, subterranean winery seemed logical, especially given the capacity to create a gravity-flow production system. The unique three-tier structure allows crushing to be done on top of the winery, and from there the juice is sent underground to the top floor. When the time is ripe, small lots of wine are sent, via one-inch hoses, a level deeper. White wines are aged in a barrel room underground; red wines mature in the adjoining cave. This system eliminates the need for pumping equipment; refrigeration is required only to cool the fermentation tanks.

The winery farms Sauvignon Blanc, Zinfandel, and Cabernet Sauvignon vineyards in the hot, arid Dry Creek Valley. Increasingly, Fritz buys Pinot Noir and Chardonnay grapes from the nearby Russian River Valley, where the cool climate regulates the ripening of the grapes, a portion of them from Dutton Ranch, known for producing some of the finest fruit in the Russian River area. Fritz Winery instituted some drastic changes in 1996, slashing annual production to twelve thousand cases from nearly thirty thousand. The figure has increased since to almost eighteen thousand. The winery is beginning to harvest some of the twenty acres of Pinot Noir acquired in the Russian River Valley in the late 1990s. When that vineyard is in full production, the winery's output will probably top out at twenty-one thousand cases. As the winery works toward this goal, the winemaker, Christina Pallmann, continues to receive professional recognition and highly coveted awards.

Visitors who troop up the hill can enjoy a view of Lake Fritz from the patio, where market umbrellas provide shade for round tables just outside the tasting room. Rockroses and other hardy plants give way to wild grasses as the hill slopes down to the water's edge.

GLORIA FERRER CHAMPAGNE CAVES

The Carneros District, with its continual winds and cool marine air, is known far and wide as an ideal climate for growing Pinot Noir and Chardonnay grapes. The word spread all the way to Spain, where the Ferrer family had been making sparkling wine for more than a century. In 1889, Pedro Ferrer founded Freixenet, now one of the world's two largest producers of sparkling wine.

Members of the family had been looking for vineyard land in the United States off and on for fifty years when José and Gloria Ferrer visited the southern part of the Sonoma Valley. The climate reminded them of their Catalan home in Spain, and in 1982, they acquired a forty-acre pasture and then, four years later, another two hundred acres nearby. They started planting vine-yards with Pinot Noir and Chardonnay, the traditional sparkling wine grapes. The winery now cultivates nearly four hundred acres in the Carneros and, in addition to sparkling wines, produces still wines, including Merlot, Pinot Noir, and Chardonnay. The wines have a history of critical success. Within a year of its 1986 debut, the winery won seven gold medals and a Sweepstakes Award at the San Francisco Fair's International Wine Competition.

The winery that José Ferrer built was the first champagne facility in the Carneros. Named for his wife, it was designed after a *masia* (a Catalan farmhouse), complete with terraces, a red tile roof, and thick walls the color of the Spanish plains. Complementing the exterior, the winery's cool interior has dark tile floors and Spanish textiles. The ties to Spain continue in the winery's shop, which offers a selection of cookbooks devoted to Spanish cuisine and the specialties of Catalonia. Also available are several Sonoma-grown products such as Gloria Ferrer's champagne-filled chocolates, mustards and dipping sauces, and a selection of table condiments.

Visitors are welcome to enjoy Gloria Ferrer wines, both still and sparkling, in the spacious tasting room or outside on the Vista Terrace. There they are treated to a breathtaking view of the Carneros District and the upper reaches of San Pablo Bay. On a clear day, they can see all the way to the peak of 3,848-foot Mount Diablo in the East Bay. Both still and sparkling wines are aged in the caves tunneled into the hill behind the hospitality center.

Tours of the winery, offered daily, include a visit to these aromatic dark recesses where guides explain the traditional *méthode champenoise* process of creating sparkling wine, during which the wine undergoes its secondary fermentation—the one that forms the characteristic bubbles—in the bottle, not in the barrel.

GLORIA FERRER CHAMPAGNE CAVES
23555 Hwy. 121
Sonoma, CA 95476
707-996-7256
info@gloriaferrer.com
www.gloriaferrer.com

OWNER: Freixenet, S.A.

LOCATION: 6 miles south of town of Sonoma.

APPELLATION: Los Carneros.

HOURS: 10 A.M.–5 P.M. daily.

TASTINGS: $4–10 per glass of sparkling wine; $1–3 for table wine.

TOURS: Daily during hours of operation.

THE WINES: Blanc de Noirs, Brut, Chardonnay, Merlot, Pinot Noir, Syrah.

SPECIALTIES: Brut Rosé, José S. Ferrer Reserve, Carneros Cuvée, Gravel Knob Vineyard Pinot Noir, Rust Rock Terrace Pinot Noir.

WINEMAKER: Bob Iantosca.

ANNUAL PRODUCTION: 120,000 cases.

OF SPECIAL NOTE: Spanish cookbooks and locally made products, as well as deli items, sold at the winery. Annual Catalan Festival (July).

NEARBY ATTRACTIONS: Mission San Francisco Solano and other historic buildings in downtown Sonoma; Infineon Raceway (NASCAR and other events); biplane flights; Cornerstone Festival of Gardens (high-concept landscape installations); Viansa Winery Wetlands (tours).

IMAGERY ESTATE WINERY

IMAGERY ESTATE WINERY
14335 Hwy. 12
Glen Ellen, CA 95442
707-935-4515
877-550-4278
info@imagerywinery.com
www.imagerywinery.com

OWNERS: Benziger family.

LOCATION: 3 miles north
of the town of Sonoma via
Hwy. 12.

APPELLATION:
Sonoma Valley.

HOURS: 10 A.M.–4:30 P.M.
daily.

TASTINGS: $5 for 5 Artist
Collection wines; $10 for
5 Vineyard Collection
wines.

TOURS: None.

THE WINES: Barbera,
Cabernet Franc, Cabernet
Sauvignon, Chardonnay,
Lagrein, Malbec, Petite
Sirah, Pinot Blanc, Port,
Sangiovese, Viognier,
White Burgundy.

SPECIALTY: Limited-
production varietals.

WINEMAKER: Joe Benziger.

ANNUAL PRODUCTION:
7,000 cases.

OF SPECIAL NOTE: Imagery
estate wines available only
in tasting room. Gallery
of 175 original artworks
commissioned by winery;
patio seating; picnic area;
bocce ball court. Limited-
edition wine-label prints
and extensive collection
of serving pieces at
winery shop.

NEARBY ATTRACTIONS:
Jack London State Historic
Park (museum, hiking,
horseback riding);
Sonoma Valley Regional
Park (hiking, dog park).

When is a wine bottle more than just a wine bottle? When it is adorned with an original work of art. This is the case for the wines in the Imagery Estate Winery's Artist Collection, each bottle of which has a distinctive label bearing artwork.

The contemporary artists commissioned to create the labels include Robert Arneson, Chester Arnold, Squeak Carnwath, Roy De Forest, Mary Frank, David Gilhooly, David Nash, Nathan Oliveira, William Wiley, and Chihung Yang. The winery itself is almost as much a gallery as it is a wine-making facility and even has its own curator, Bob Nugent, a recognized artist with strong ties to the national art com-munity. Nugent has organized the 175 pieces of original label art into a permanent display in the hospitality center. Like the winemaking facility behind it, the hospitality center is in an earth-toned modern building that is surprisingly compatible with the bucolic Sonoma Valley.

The most important artist at Imagery Estate Winery, however, is Joe Benziger. A member of the acclaimed family that runs the nearby Benziger Family Winery, Joe Benziger has been the creative force behind the Imagery wines since their inception. He handles every detail of the winery's two tiers, the Artist Collection and the Vineyard Collection. The Artist Collection is known for its limited quantities of uncommon varietal offerings, such as Petite Sirah and Malbec. The newer Vineyard Collection features only select, single-vineyard wines from exceptional vineyards throughout Sonoma County appellations.

The original Artist Collection dates to 1985, when the owners of Benziger Family Winery and Imagery Estate Winery found themselves with two small lots of exceptional Chardonnay and Zinfandel. The challenge was to find a way to showcase wines that were too limited to market nationally but too special to ignore. As serendipity would have it, winemaker Joe Benziger happened to meet Bob Nugent at a local polo match. That encounter led to Nugent's creation of a wine label. By the second vintage, the concept evolved as a way to focus on esoteric grape varietals not readily available in most winery offerings.

The Imagery Estate wines became so popular that in the summer of 2000, the family moved the entire operation, including the winemaking facilities and the artwork, to their property on Highway 12, less than two miles from the Benziger Family Winery. This is where visitors now come to taste the wines and linger to admire the art collection, the largest of its kind in the United States.

J VINEYARDS & WINERY

J Vineyards & Winery was among the first California wineries to create a pairing menu to serve with its wines in the tasting room. The winery's philosophy is to enhance the visitor's experience of wine as a beverage that belongs on the table. Chef Mark Caldwell carefully crafts these menus to demonstrate wine's natural affinity for a variety of foods, using local artisanal sources in his recipes whenever possible.

The list of wines and foods changes frequently, but always includes at least one sparkling wine and one Pinot Noir. A typical menu matches Vintage Brut with Dungeness crab, cilantro-serrano crème fraîche, and avocado in phyllo; Pinot Gris with poached shrimp and roasted Meyer lemon vinaigrette; Pinot Noir with Reyes blue cheese feuilletes; and wild mushroom and spinach frittata.  sautéed heirloom chicories and Point Nicole's Vineyard Pinot Noir with J Vineyards & Winery conducts these pairings at a twenty-six-foot-long bar of glass and acid-washed steel that extends across the back of the spacious tasting room. Behind it is a large, eye-catching wall in which bubbles appear to be rising, created with jagged glass and fiber optics. Both pieces were specially designed by artist Gordon Heuther and installed in time for the winery's 1999 opening.

In 2003 J took the concept to a higher level when the adjacent Bubble Room reserve tasting salon made its debut. In this elegant but comfortable combination of living room and dining room, several rectangular tables as well as armchairs and love seats afford a number of seating options. Visitors select from among three choices: a flight of four sparkling wines paired with caviars; a white flight of sparkling wine, Viognier, and two Chardonnays served with dishes such as a spicy crab wonton; and a red flight of four wines (including three Pinot Noirs) paired with meatier fare such as Kobe beef chili with crème fraîche or spicy seared Muscovy duck breast.

When Judy Jordan founded J Vineyards & Winery, she envisioned a *méthode champenoise* facility devoted to a single product made from the high-quality Chardonnay and Pinot Noir that thrive in the Russian River Valley. J Vintage Brut remains the winery's signature, accounting for half of its production, but the J family of wines has grown to include several still wines. The majority of the estate's 250 vineyard acres are planted with Pinot Noir. The remainder consist mostly of Chardonnay and Pinot Gris.

J Vineyards & Winery continues to refine its original game plan. It has begun to produce two aperitif beverages: J Pear Liqueur and Ratafia Dessert Wine. Either would make a perfect ending to any tasting.

J VINEYARDS & WINERY
11447 Old Redwood Hwy.
Healdsburg, CA 95448
707-431-3646
winefolk@jwine.com
www.jwine.com

OWNER: Judy Jordan.

LOCATION: About 3 miles south of Healdsburg.

APPELLATION: Russian River Valley.

HOURS: 11 A.M.–5 P.M. daily; Bubble Room, 11 A.M.–4 P.M. Friday–Monday.

TASTINGS: $20 for 4 pairings in tasting room; $45 for 4 pairings in Bubble Room.

TOURS: By appointment.

THE WINES: Chardonnay, Pinot Gris, Pinot Noir, Pinotage, Viognier, Zinfandel.

SPECIALTIES: Pinot Noir, sparkling wine.

WINEMAKER: Oded Shakked.

ANNUAL PRODUCTION: 70,000 cases.

OF SPECIAL NOTE: Annual events include Winter Wineland (January), Barrel Tasting (March), Wine & Food Affair (November). Chardonnay, Pinotage, and Viognier available only at winery.

NEARBY ATTRACTIONS: Russian River (swimming; canoe and kayak rentals); hot-air balloon rides.

JORDAN VINEYARD & WINERY

JORDAN VINEYARD & WINERY
1474 Alexander Valley Rd.
Healdsburg, CA 95448
707-431-5250
800-654-1213
info@jordanwinery.com
www.jordanwinery.com

OWNER: Thomas Jordan.

LOCATION: About 4 miles
northeast of Healdsburg
via Hwy. 128.

APPELLATION:
Alexander Valley.

HOURS: 9 A.M.–5 P.M.
Monday–Friday; 9 A.M.–
4 P.M. Saturday. Open
Sundays June–December.

TASTINGS: By appointment
with tours. Complimentary
tastings of current releases.

TOURS: By appointment,
at 11 A.M. and 1 P.M.
Monday–Saturday.

THE WINES: Cabernet
Sauvignon, Chardonnay.

SPECIALTIES: Alexander
Valley Cabernet Sauvignon,
Russian River Chardonnay.

WINEMAKER: Rob Davis.

ANNUAL PRODUCTION:
90,000 cases.

OF SPECIAL NOTE: Extensive
landscaped grounds and
gardens, including Tuscan
olive trees. Jordan olive
oil sold at winery. Library,
dessert, and large-format
wines available only
at winery.

NEARBY ATTRACTIONS:
Lake Sonoma (boating,
camping, hiking); Jimtown
Store (country market,
homemade foods).

P arts of Sonoma County resemble the French wine country, but mostly in a topographical sense. The picture always lacked a key element: a grand château. That changed in 1976, when Tom Jordan established his 1,500-acre estate on an oak-studded knoll in the Alexander Valley.

Inspired by several eighteenth-century châteaus in southwestern France, the winery was designed by the San Francisco architectural firm of Backen, Arrigoni & Ross. The building, with its classic facade of golden yellow plaster finish, clay-tile roof, and wine-red doors and shutters, also serves as a visual metaphor for the winemaking philosophy at Jordan, where Cabernet Sauvignon is blended in the Bordeaux style and Chardonnay is crafted in the time-honored tradition of a white Burgundy.

As visitors approach on the winding driveway, they are teased with glimpses of the château until they reach the top of the hill and can finally see the entire structure and its landscaped grounds. The image of an old-world estate is furthered by the formal French gardens with their clipped privet hedges, poplar trees, and pollarded sycamores. Boston ivy clinging to the château walls changes colors with the seasons, creating a subdued kaleidoscope that softens the look of the exterior. Gracing the entrance is a small bronze statue of Bacchus, a copy of Jacopo Sansovino Tatti's 1512 original in the National Museum in Florence. From the hilltop, virtually every vantage affords panoramic vistas of the Alexander Valley and its most dramatic focal points, Geyser Peak and Mount St. Helena. It was ancient volcanic activity from Geyser Peak, along with eons of seismic uplift, that formed the narrow, twenty-mile-long valley named for the pioneering family who began farming this area in 1847.

The land Tom Jordan acquired in 1972 included 275 acres for vineyards and another 1,300 acres of rolling oak woodlands, plus two lakes. There would be plenty of room for a winery facility as well as an informal preserve for deer, wild turkeys, coyotes, waterfowl, and other wildlife. In 1995 Jordan began planting a grove of Tuscan olive trees that now produce fruit for the winery's award-winning organic extra-virgin olive oil.

Tours at Jordan wend their way along a path with sweeping views of hillside vineyards, olive groves, and an organic vegetable and flower garden. Winemaking is then covered in some detail in the production facility. Each tour culminates with a tasting of current releases in the comfortable library where guests are invited to linger. Tom Jordan's wife, Sandra, who has her own line of home decor, designed many of the furnishings in the room, including a wine table modeled on an eighteenth-century piece.

KENWOOD VINEYARDS

The photogenic, century-old barn where visitors come to taste Kenwood's wines dates to one of the most romantic eras in Sonoma Valley history. The quintessential adventure author Jack London was living, writing, and raising grapes in nearby Glen Ellen when the Pagani Brothers established their winery in 1906 in the buildings that now house Kenwood Vineyards. In those days, long before the invention of tasting rooms, wine lovers would bring their own barrels and jugs to be filled and then cart them home.

Decades later, in 1970, a trio of wine enthusiasts from the San Francisco Bay Area founded

Kenwood Vineyards. In redesigning and modernizing the existing winery, they created a facility that allows the winemaker the utmost in flexibility. More than 125 stainless steel ferment-ing and upright oak tanks are utilized in combination with some seventeen thousand French and American oak barrels. Kenwood uses estate fruit as well as grapes from some of Sonoma County's best vineyards and follows the *cuvée* winemaking method, in which the harvest from each vineyard is handled separately to preserve its individual character. According to winemaker Michael Lee, one of the winery's founders, such "small lot" winemaking allows each lot of grapes to be brought to its fullest potential before blending. Likewise, the acclaimed Artist Series is a masterful blend of the top barrels of Cabernet Sauvignon.

The historic barn and other original buildings lend a nostalgic ambience to the modern winemaking facilities on the twenty-two-acre estate. But there is another link to the romantic history of the Valley of the Moon, as author London dubbed Sonoma Valley.

Best known for his rugged individualism and dynamic writing, London was also an accomplished farmer and rancher. At the heart of his Beauty Ranch—now part of the Jack London State Historic Park—several hundred acres of vineyards were planted in the 1870s on terraced slopes. The volcanic ash fields produced excellent wines by the turn of the twentieth century. London died in 1916, and by World War II, his crop fields had become overgrown. But in 1976, Kenwood Vineyards became the exclusive marketer of wines produced from the ranch. The Cabernet Sauvignon, Zinfandel, Merlot, and Pinot Noir, made only from Jack London vineyard grapes, bear a label with the image of a wolf's head, London's signature stamp.

Known for consistency of quality in both its red and its white wines, Kenwood produces mostly moderately priced wines. The major exception is the Artist Series Cabernet Sauvignons, which have been collector's items since first released in 1978.

KENWOOD VINEYARDS
9592 Hwy. 12
Kenwood, CA 95452
707-833-5891
info@heckestates.com
www.kenwoodvineyards.com

OWNER: F. Korbel & Bros.

LOCATION: 15 miles southeast of Santa Rosa on Hwy. 12.

APPELLATION: Sonoma Valley.

HOURS: 10 A.M.–4:30 P.M. daily.

TASTINGS: Complimentary; $5 for Private Reserve wines.

TOURS: None.

THE WINES: Cabernet Sauvignon, Chardonnay, Gewürztraminer, Merlot, Pinot Noir, Sauvignon Blanc, sparkling wines, White Zinfandel, Zinfandel.

SPECIALTIES: Artist Series, Jack London Ranch wines.

WINEMAKER: Pat Henderson.

ANNUAL PRODUCTION: 550,000 cases.

OF SPECIAL NOTE: Monthly themed food-and-wine events matching chef's specialties with appropriate wines. Limited-release Artist Series wines available only at winery.

NEARBY ATTRACTIONS: Jack London State Historic Park (museum, hiking, horseback riding); Sugarloaf Ridge State Park (hiking, camping, horseback riding).

LAMBERT BRIDGE WINERY

LAMBERT BRIDGE WINERY
4085 West Dry Creek Rd.
Healdsburg, CA 95448
707-431-9600,
800-975-0555
wines@lambertbridge.com
www.lambertbridge.com

OWNERS: Patti Chambers
and managing partner
Greg Wilcox.

LOCATION: About 6.5 miles
northwest of Healdsburg
via Dry Creek Rd.

APPELLATION: Dry Creek
Valley.

HOURS: 10:30 A.M.–4:30 P.M.
daily.

TASTINGS: $5 for 6 wines;
$10 for 6 reserve wines.

TOURS: By appointment.

THE WINES:
30th Anniversary Cuvée,
Cabernet Franc, Cabernet
Sauvignon, Chardonnay,
Crane Creek Cuvée,
Merlot, Petit Sirah,
Sauvignon Blanc, Syrah,
Viognier, Zinfandel.

SPECIALTY: Bordeaux
varietals.

WINEMAKER: Jill Davis.

ANNUAL PRODUCTION:
10,000 cases.

OF SPECIAL NOTE: Picnic
tables and gardens;
seasonal cooking and edu-
cational classes. Annual
events include Passport to
Dry Creek Valley (April),
Harvest Festival (October),
Thanksgiving Open House
(November). Bottle limits
on Cabernet Franc, Crane
Creek Cuvée, Maple
Zinfandel, and Rockpile
Zinfandel.

NEARBY ATTRACTIONS:
Lake Sonoma (boating,
camping, hiking).

Surrounded by the lush vineyards and rolling hills of the Dry Creek Valley, Lambert Bridge Winery offers a setting for all seasons. In spring, the hillside is yellow with daffodils. By summer, the decades-old wisteria vines clinging to the porch roof render a profusion of aromatic lavender blossoms. From then until late fall, the weather is perfect for picnicking in the Mediterranean-style gardens. And as winter's wet chill descends on Dry Creek Valley, a roaring blaze in a huge granite hearth fills the high-ceilinged tasting room with welcoming warmth.

The site once belonged to the C. L. Lambert Ranch, a large parcel that included farmland as well as a 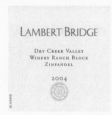 school, a store, and a trestle bridge across Dry Creek. The Lambert Bridge, which dates to 1920, is now the only single-lane, public bridge in the valley. Lambert Bridge Winery, which opened in 1975, is only the second winery to be built in Dry Creek Valley since Prohibition.

Bordeaux varietals and blends take center stage in the winery's ten-thousand-case portfolio. The winemaking team is headed by veteran winemaker Jill Davis, whose twenty-six years of experience include stints at Beringer, Buena Vista, and William Hill. Davis works side by side with Mitch Fire-stone-Gillis, who has been making wine for twenty-five years, most recently at the Williams Selyem Winery. The newest member to join the team is consulting winemaker Heidi Barrett of Screaming Eagle Winery. It is unusual for such a small winery to boast a team of veteran winemakers who, between them, represent more than seventy-five years of experience. Davis, Firestone-Gillis, and Barrett apply their extensive knowledge of limited-production, artisan-style winemaking techniques to make fifteen different wines in handcrafted small lots, using mostly fruit from estate vineyards.

Starting with the harvest of 2005, Lambert Bridge began using an elaborate new collection of technologically advanced equipment that allows the sorting and selection of wine grapes down to the individual berries. Only completely mature, perfectly formed grapes are hand-selected for the wines. The process is so time-intensive that few wineries use it, but Lambert Bridge finds that the improvement in quality more than justifies the extra effort.

The tasting room features a redwood bar fronted in hand-hammered copper. It is a close match to the twelve-foot-long reserve tasting bar in the adjacent barrel room. Here soaring redwood ceilings and glowing candlelight establish a fitting ambience for sampling limited-production wines. The winery's extensively landscaped picnic grounds and gardens are home to the imported wood-fired ovens in the Mugnaini Al Fresco Kitchen. Internationally acclaimed chef Andrea Mugnaini demon-strates her culinary talents at the winery in a series of cooking classes and wine education events.

LANCASTER ESTATE

A small, family-owned winery, Lancaster Estate was founded in 1995 with the goal of producing only the finest estate-grown Cabernet-based wines. Located beside the narrow and less-traveled roads of southern Alexander Valley, the winery evokes the rich agricultural heritage of this acclaimed appellation.

This off-the-beaten-path region in the foothills of the western Mayacamas Range is blessed with a favorable growing climate consisting of warm days and cool nights, and a complex composition of soil types—ideal conditions for growing wines of quality and distinction. Lancaster Estate consists of seventy-two acres in total, with fifty-three acres planted exclusively to the classic Bordeaux varietals—Cabernet Sauvignon, Cabernet Franc Merlot, Malbec, and Petit Verdot.

Visitors enter the estate driveway from twisting, two-lane Chalk Hill Road and are immediately treated to views of gently rolling hillside vineyards and majestic oaks. Guests, who are welcome by appointment only, get a close look at the property, from grapevines to wine tasting, during their approximately ninety-minute visit. First, they are chauffeured—in groups of up to four—around the vineyards in the estate SUV. Then they are escorted to the winery's nine-thousand-square-foot underground cave, where Lancaster Estate ages its wines for twenty-two months in French oak barrels in a naturally controlled setting that maintains the perfect temperature and humidity conditions. Here, guests learn about the estate's growing practices, its production techniques, and its philosophy of aging wines as gently as possible.

A niche has been carved out of the cave's southern wall to create an intimate library, a dramatically decorated room where halogen lights beam down on a tall circular table. More than seven hundred bottles of wine, representing every vintage since 1996, are stored along one wall within arm's reach. Although the library is reserved for VIP tastings, visitors are welcome to take a peek—and even a photograph or two.

The tour, which is complimentary for up to ten people, concludes with a tasting of three current-release wines in the châteaulike hospitality center, where dark green awnings and climbing vines frame the building's stylish ocher facade. Inside, guests discover a salon setting where the full-length curtains and upholstered love seats echo the terra-cotta and gold color scheme of the Lancaster family crest.

LANCASTER ESTATE
15001 Chalk Hill Rd.
Healdsburg, CA 95448
707-433-8178
hospitality@lancaster-estate.com
www.lancaster-estate.com

OWNERS: Ted and Nicole Simpkins.

LOCATION: Less than 11 miles east of Healdsburg via Alexander Valley Rd.

APPELLATION: Alexander Valley.

HOURS: 10 A.M.–4 P.M. Monday–Saturday.

TASTINGS: By appointment. Complimentary for up to 10 people. $20 per person thereafter. Features 3 current release wines.

TOURS: By appointment. Complimentary vineyard and winery tour for up to 10 people. $20 per person thereafter.

THE WINE: Cabernet Sauvignon.

SPECIALTY: Cabernet Sauvignon.

WINEMAKER: Jennifer Higgins.

ANNUAL PRODUCTION: 4,250 cases.

OF SPECIAL NOTE: Annual events available by invitation only. Lancaster Estate Nicole's Proprietary Red Wine (250 cases produced) and other limited-release wines available only at the winery.

NEARBY ATTRACTIONS: Lake Sonoma (boating, camping, hiking); Jimtown Store (country market, homemade foods).

LEDSON WINERY AND VINEYARDS

LEDSON WINERY AND VINEYARDS
7335 Hwy. 12
Kenwood, CA 95409
707-537-3810
www.ledson.com

OWNER:
Steve Noble Ledson.

LOCATION: About 2 miles northwest of Kenwood.

APPELLATION:
Sonoma Valley.

HOURS: 10 A.M.–5 P.M. daily.

TASTINGS: $5 for 5 wines.

TOURS: Self-guided.

THE WINES: Barbera, Cabernet Franc, Cabernet Sauvignon, Chardonnay, Grenache, Malbec, Merlot, Mourvèdre, Orange Muscat, Petite Sirah, Pinot Noir, Port, Primitivo, Riesling, Rosé, Sangiovese, Sauvignon Blanc, Syrah, Zinfandel.

SPECIALTIES: Small lots of handcrafted Merlot, Chardonnay, Cabernet Sauvignon, and Zinfandel.

WINEMAKER:
Steve Noble Ledson.

ANNUAL PRODUCTION:
35,000 cases.

OF SPECIAL NOTE: Ledson wines available only at winery and online store. Market offering gourmet foods; dinner by reservation; food-and-wine pairing program. Six-room Ledson Hotel & Harmony Club, in the town of Sonoma on Sonoma Plaza, includes a wine bar and has the same distinctive charm as the winery.

NEARBY ATTRACTIONS:
Sugarloaf State Park (hiking, camping, horseback riding); Annadel State Park (hiking, biking).

It came to be known as "the castle"—the Gothic edifice that took ten years and some two million bricks to create. As people drove up and down the highway in front of it, they wondered if it was a house or an elegant winery. When the Ledson family started construction in 1989, they thought the property would be ideal for their residence. They planted Merlot and Zinfandel vineyards and began work on the house. As the months passed, the turrets, slate roofs, balconies, and fountains took shape, and passersby would even climb over the fences to get a better look.

Steve Ledson finally realized it was time to rethink his plan. Given the intense public interest in the building and the quality of his grape harvests—which he sold to nearby wineries—he decided to turn the sixteen-thousand-square-foot structure into a winery and tasting room. In 1997 he released the winery's first wine: the 1994 Estate Merlot. After two years of reconstruction, the winery opened in 1999.

Fortunately, Ledson not only had his own construction company but also benefited from his family's history of farming in the area, beginning in the 1860s. His grandmother's father was an early pioneer in Sonoma County winemaking, and both sets of grandparents had worked their adjoining Sonoma Valley ranches cooperatively. Eventually, this Ledson acreage became part of Annadel State Park. Steve Ledson, the fifth generation to farm in the area, had always wanted to grow grapes, and when he had the chance, he bought the twenty-one-acre property—which just happened to have a view of Annadel park.

Visitors to the castle today find an estate worthy of the French countryside, with a grand brick driveway, a manicured landscape, and a flourishing collection of roses. Just inside the front door is a huge curved staircase and three spacious rooms for tasting and shopping. The curious will delight in finding remnants of the original architecture, such as mini-Gothic fireplaces in the retail shop. The interior was designed entirely by Steve Ledson and features ornate wood inlays and mosaics created by son Mike.

At Ledson, visitors have a myriad of dining choices. They can enjoy a picnic lunch served outdoors on tables overlooking the estate vineyards and fountains, or assemble their own picnic from the Gourmet Marketplace, which features a tempting selection of gourmet meats, artisan cheeses, and fresh made-to-order sandwiches, as well as salads and desserts. For special events, guests may arrange to have intimate dinners in the castle's parlor. With its elegant Italian marble fireplaces and breathtaking views, the room is cozy and inviting.

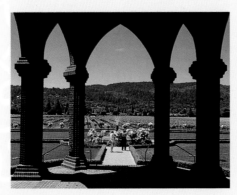

MATANZAS CREEK WINERY

Every spring and summer, the lavender fields at Matanzas Creek Winery in Bennett Valley burst into fragrant blossoms that envelop the entire estate in an invisible, sweet-smelling mist. As beautiful as they are, the lavender fields occupy only a fraction of the property.

Founded in 1977, Matanzas Creek Winery is located on the site of a former dairy farm in Sonoma County's picturesque Bennett Valley. In 1985 the original winery, a converted dairy barn, gave way to a modern winemaking facility, and since that time the estate's Bennett Valley vineyards have been expanded to include more than 280 acres of Chardonnay, Merlot, and Syrah. In addition to these grapes, vineyard acquisitions in Sonoma Valley, Carneros, Russian River Valley, and Knights Valley provide the winemakers with an extensive selection of Sauvignon Blanc and Syrah fruit for craft-ing their wines.

As important as the win-ery's history is its location in Bennett Valley, one of the new-est American Viticultural Areas (AVA) in Sonoma County. Once defined as part of the county's Sonoma Valley and Sonoma Mountain AVAs, Bennett Valley overlaps with these regions but carves out 8,150 acres to call its own (of which 850 acres are planted with grapevines). The appellation was formalized only in December 2003, but Bennett Valley's exceptionally hospitable grape-growing environment was first discovered back in the mid-1800s. Until thirty years ago, however, the region was better known for the dairy farms and apple orchards established by the first American settlers. Surrounded by Taylor Mountain to the west, Sonoma Mountain to the south, and Bennett Peak to the east, the valley is cooled by coastal fog and breezes that drift northeast through the Crane Canyon gap and provide a long growing season that creates complex characteristics. The vines also benefit from a diversity of soil types, including deposits of ash on the valley floor from the volcanic peaks, as well as basalt, an ancient ocean-floor rock that imparts a slightly smoky character to the Matanzas Creek Merlot.

When the winery was founded in 1977, it was named after a nearby stream called Matanzas by the early Spanish for the Pomo Indian deer hunts that were once common in the area. It remains one of the few tasting rooms in the entire valley. Visitors are entranced with the extravagant, terraced perennial gardens. Throughout the year, they can shop for souvenirs of the estate's lavender plants in the form of handcrafted soaps, lotions, and other toiletries, as well as a line of lavender-influenced culinary products including lavender grilling hay, honey, salt, and a collection of spice rubs to pair with specific wine varietals.

MATANZAS CREEK WINERY
6097 Bennett Valley Rd.
Santa Rosa, CA 95404
707-528-6464
800-590-6464
info@matanzascreek.com
www.matanzascreek.com

OWNERS: Jess Jackson and Barbara Banke.

LOCATION: About 6 miles southeast of Santa Rosa via Bennett Valley Rd.

APPELLATIONS: Bennett Valley and Sonoma Valley.

HOURS: 10 A.M.–4:30 P.M. daily.

TASTING: $5 for 4 or 5 wines.

TOURS: By appointment. 10:30 A.M. and 2:30 P.M. Monday–Friday and 10:30 A.M. Saturday.

THE WINES: Cabernet Sauvignon, Chardonnay, Merlot, Sauvignon Blanc, Syrah.

SPECIALTY: Merlot.

WINEMAKER: François Cordesse.

ANNUAL PRODUCTION: 40,000–45,000 cases.

OF SPECIAL NOTE: Picnic area beneath oak trees with vineyard views. Gift shop featuring soap, sachets, grilling sticks, and other items made from estate-grown lavender. Proprietor's Blend (Merlot based), Rosé, and Port available only at winery.

NEARBY ATTRACTIONS: Luther Burbank Garden and Home (tours of famed horticulturist's property); Charles M. Schulz Museum (exhibits on Peanuts creator and other cartoonists).

RAVENSWOOD WINERY

RAVENSWOOD WINERY
18701 Gehricke Rd.
Sonoma, CA 95476
707-938-1960
888-669-4679
rwwine@ravenswood-wine.com
www.ravenswood-wine.com

OWNER: Constellation Brands.

LOCATION: About .5 mile northeast of the town of Sonoma via Fourth St. East and Lovall Valley Rd.

APPELLATION: Sonoma Valley.

HOURS: 10 A.M.–4:30 P.M. daily.

TASTINGS: $5 for 5 wines; $10 for reserve wines.

TOURS: 10:30 A.M. daily, by appointment.

THE WINES: Bordeaux-style blends, Cabernet Franc, Cabernet Sauvignon, Chardonnay, ICON (Rhône-style blend), Merlot, Petite Sirah, Zinfandel.

SPECIALTY: Zinfandel.

WINEMAKER: Joel Peterson.

ANNUAL PRODUCTION: 500,000 cases.

OF SPECIAL NOTE: Blending seminars by appointment. Bicyclists and other visitors are welcome to picnic on stone patio with view of vineyards.

NEARBY ATTRACTIONS: Mission San Francisco Solano and other historic buildings in downtown Sonoma; bike rentals; Vella Cheese Company; Sonoma Cheese Factory; Sonoma Traintown (rides on a scale railroad).

Few wineries set out to make cult wines, and probably fewer earn a widespread following as well. Ravenswood has done both. Its founders began by crushing enough juice to make 327 cases of Zinfandel in 1976, and although the winery also makes other wines, Zinfandel remains king. Nearly three-quarters of Ravenswood's production is Zinfandel.

Winemaker and cofounder Joel Peterson and chairman and cofounder Reed Foster were so successful with that first, handcrafted vintage that they have had to live up to the standard it set ever since. Ravenswood produces fourteen different Zinfandels that represent the spectrum of the varietal's personality, with tastes ranging from peppery and spicy to chocolaty and minty. If there is one common denominator, it is reflected in the slogan adopted by the winery in 1990: "No Wimpy Wines."

Most of Ravenswood's grapes come from more than a hundred independent growers. It is those long-standing relationships that ensure the consistency of the wines. One vineyard source dates to 1986. The Strotz family invited Joel Peterson to visit their Sonoma Mountain vineyard, which they had named Pickberry because of all the wild blackberries harvested there. Peterson immediately recognized the quality of the Strotz grapes, and in 1988, Ravenswood released the first of its many blends of Cabernet Sauvignon, Cabernet Franc, and Merlot under the vineyard-designated name Pickberry.

Peterson never set out to specialize in Zinfandel; originally he was more interested in the Bordeaux varietals he began tasting at the age of ten with his father, Walter, founder of the San Francisco Wine Sampling Club. In time, however, he fell under the spell of Zinfandel. In the 1970s, after a brief career as a wine writer and consultant, he went to work for the late Joseph Swan, considered one of California's outstanding craftsmen of fine Zinfandel. Thus the stage was set for the varietal's ascendancy at the winery Peterson founded.

Ravenswood farms fourteen acres of estate vineyards on the northeast side of Sonoma. The old stone building, once home to the Haywood Winery, has extensive patio seating with beautiful south-facing views of the vineyards. Thanks to the company's growth, the winemaking operations have since been relocated to a forty-five-thousand-square-foot facility in the Carneros, to the south, but the tasting room remains. Originally a cozy, even cramped affair, it was greatly expanded in 1996, and now has plenty of elbow room as well as ample natural light for visitors who come to sample and appreciate the wines.

RAYMOND BURR VINEYARDS

In 1986, some thirty years after the hit television show *Perry Mason* made Raymond Burr a household name, the actor decided to follow another passion: making great wine. The small Dry Creek Valley estate that bears his name does not produce enough grapes to find the worldwide audience of a hit TV series, but its reputation is growing.

Burr met fellow actor Robert Benevides on the set of *Perry Mason,* and they soon discovered that they shared an interest in appreciating wine and growing orchids. Eventually, the two friends turned both hobbies into viable commercial operations. In 1976 Benevides purchased forty prime acres of benchland at the foot of Bradford Mountain west of Healdsburg. As Burr's series *Ironside* was ending its eight-year run, the actor got his first look at the ranch. He must have been pleased: the view from the east-facing slopes of the property takes in a scenic swath of countryside, with hills and manzanita trees as far as the eye can see. In 1980 they relocated the commercial orchid nursery established several years earlier to the ranch and began developing the property.

The intimate, bungalow-style tasting room is filled with memorabilia from Raymond Burr's acting career, notably his Emmy awards and vintage issues of *TV Guide* with his picture on the covers. The space is cozy, so unless the weather is dismal, visitors take their glasses out to the patio, where they can be served in the shade of an old oak tree and take in the sweeping views. Sensational orchids can be seen in the greenhouses year-round, but fall is peak bloom season.

The fourteen-acre vineyard is on a steeply terraced hillside with very well-drained soil, ideal conditions for premium Cabernet Sauvignon grapes. Although the Dry Creek Valley is a warm growing region, the east-facing vineyards are bathed in shade late in the day, and the cool air from the nearby ocean keeps the temperatures low at night. The combination allows the grapes to mature at a steady pace. The longer the fruit hangs on the vine, the more flavor it develops. As John Quinones, who joined Raymond Burr Vineyards as winemaker in 1998, says, "A winemaker can't create quality. It's our job to preserve and enhance what comes out of the vineyard." Currently the vineyard includes eight acres of Cabernet Sauvignon, four acres of Chardonnay, and two acres of Cabernet Franc. Sadly, Burr's health deteriorated as the vineyards thrived, and he passed away in 1993. But a comment he made in a documentary about Northern California wines reflected his thinking about the vital, even intimate relationship between grape grower and land: "The most important things in a vineyard are the footprints of the grower between the rows."

RAYMOND BURR VINEYARDS
8339 West Dry Creek Rd.
Healdsburg, CA 95448
707-433-8559
RBurrwine@aol.com
www.raymondburrvineyards.com

OWNER: Robert Benevides.

LOCATION: 8.5 miles west of Healdsburg via Dry Creek Rd. and Yoakim Bridge Rd.

APPELLATION: Dry Creek Valley.

HOURS: 11 A.M.–5 P.M. daily.

TASTINGS: Complimentary.

TOURS: None of winery.

THE WINES: Cabernet Franc, Cabernet Sauvignon, Chardonnay.

SPECIALTY: Hillside Vineyard Cabernet Sauvignon.

WINEMAKER: John Quinones.

ANNUAL PRODUCTION: 3,000 cases.

OF SPECIAL NOTE: Orchid greenhouse tours on Saturdays and Sundays by appointment with minimum of 8 guests; picnic area with view of Dry Creek Valley; monthly food-and-wine tastings.

NEARBY ATTRACTIONS: Lake Sonoma (boating, camping, hiking).

SCHUG CARNEROS ESTATE WINERY

**SCHUG CARNEROS
ESTATE WINERY**
602 Bonneau Rd.
Sonoma, CA 95476
707-939-9363
800-966-9365
schug@schugwinery.com
www.schugwinery.com

OWNERS: Walter and
Gertrud Schug.

LOCATION: .5 mile west of
intersection of Hwy. 121
and Hwy. 116.

APPELLATION: Los Carneros.

HOURS: 10 A.M.–5 P.M. daily.

TASTINGS: Complimentary;
$5 for reserve wines

TOURS: By appointment.

THE WINES: Cabernet
Sauvignon, Chardonnay,
Merlot, Pinot Noir,
Sauvignon Blanc,
Sparkling Pinot Noir.

SPECIALTY: Pinot Noir.

WINEMAKER: Michael Cox.

ANNUAL PRODUCTION: More
than 20,000 cases.

OF SPECIAL NOTE: Open
house in late April and in
mid-November (Holiday
in Carneros). *Pétanque*
court open to public.

NEARBY ATTRACTIONS:
Mission San Francisco
Solano and other historic
buildings in downtown
Sonoma; Infineon Raceway
(NASCAR and other
events); biplane flights;
Cornerstone Festival of
Gardens (high-concept
landscape installations);
Viansa Winery Wetlands
(tours).

Fog and wind from the Pacific Ocean and San Francisco Bay sweep along the low, rocky hills of the Carneros appellation, where the volcanic soil, laden with clay, is shallow and dense. Grape growers intent on producing Cabernet Sauvignon and many other premium varietals avoid these conditions at all costs. But Walter Schug wanted to grow Pinot Noir, and he knew that this challenging combination of climate and geology would bring out the best in his favorite grape.

Schug first made his reputation in the 1970s as the acclaimed winemaker for Joseph Phelps. Working at the ultrapremium Napa Valley winery, he was successful with a range of wine grapes, notably Cabernet Sauvignon, before turning his attention to Pinot Noir. In 1980, beginning with grapes from a vineyard he had used at Phelps, Schug launched his own brand.

Schug and his wife, Gertrud, selected a fifty-acre site in the southern Sonoma Valley for their new vineyard estate and crowned the hilltop with a winery in 1990. They favored post-and-beam architecture reminiscent of Germany's Rhine River Valley, where the Schug family had long produced Pinot Noir. The style makes it one of the most instantly recognizable wineries in the appellation. Pinot Noir and Chardonnay vineyards surround the winery, and Schug has long-term contracts with other growers in the Carneros to ensure the best grapes year after year. Protecting and enhancing the varietal and regional characteristics of the fruit are the essence of the Schug family's philosophy.

The European aspect of the Schug estate was enhanced with the excavation of an underground cave system in the mid-1990s. The system's naturally stable temperatures and humidity levels allow the wines to age gracefully in French oak barrels. Almost every inch of the caves is covered with gray concrete, but an exposed patch at the end of one tunnel affords a glimpse of the pockmarked, pumicelike volcanic rock characteristic of the region.

Visitors are warmly welcomed at this family-managed winery. From the hilltop tasting room, they are treated to spectacular views of the surrounding countryside and the northern reaches of San Francisco Bay. Nearby is a *pétanque* court, another nod to the Schugs' European ancestry. Newcomers and old hands alike are encouraged to play this French game, which requires dexterity in tossing a small ball to exactly the right spot. More than merely a sport, *pétanque* is a pastime that invites conviviality and conversation in the best old-world tradition.

VALLEY OF THE MOON WINERY

If there's one undertaking more difficult than building a winery from scratch, it is transforming a historic winery into a facility capable of turning out first-rate wines. In 1997, that was the challenge facing the new owners of a winery established in 1863. Gary Heck, who also owns Korbel Champagne Cellars and Kenwood Vineyards, was determined to maintain the character of the original buildings. The decision to honor the winery's heritage found expression in an extensive renovation that kept the original stone walls of the winery and fermentation building and preserved the estate's old-vine Zinfandel vineyards and its landmark four-hundred-year-old bay tree.

Heck decided to build a new winemaking facility next to the original fermentation room, which was designated for a new tasting room. The first task was to uncover the twenty-seven-ton, twenty-inch-thick stone walls built in 1863 by Chinese stone masons who stayed on in the Sonoma Valley after their work on the railroads was completed. Preserving the winery's unreinforced walls, buried beneath decades of piecemeal additions, was particularly delicate work since they had to be braced to withstand earthquakes. When it came to the exterior of the new winery facility, the architect showed respect for the agricultural setting by using materials such as board and batten with metal roofs. For the color palette, the designers had to look no further than the old vines that turn red and gold in autumn. The exterior of the tasting room was plastered with a three-color, hand-troweled finish. Zinclike metal roofs, sliding barn doors, open trusses, and other early California construction details unite the new building complex.

The winery land was once part of the 48,000-acre Agua Caliente Land Grant owned by General Mariano Vallejo. In 1863 the "Stone Tract" portion was conveyed to George Whitman, the first owner to grow grapes and build a winery. Years later, the property was purchased by Senator George Hearst, father of newspaper magnate William Randolph Hearst. Senator Hearst further developed Madrone Vineyards, as it was then called, into a serious winemaking operation.

Visitors today taste wines in an 1,800-square-foot room that a century ago was filled with concrete fermentation tanks. Given rich texture with stone, metal, and hand-colored concrete, the tasting room has oversized casement windows that open out to the old-vine Zinfandel vineyard. A graceful, curvilinear wine bar is sheathed in a metal quilt of bronze, copper, and stainless steel—the same dimpled stainless steel used for the winery's steel fermentation tanks. Visible behind the tasting bar is one of the original stone walls.

VALLEY OF THE MOON WINERY
777 Madrone Rd.
Glen Ellen, CA 95442
707-996-6941
luna@vomwinery.com
www.valleyofthemoon
winery.com

OWNER: Gary Heck.

LOCATION: 5 miles north of the town of Sonoma via Hwy. 12.

APPELLATION: Sonoma Valley.

HOURS: 10 A.M.–4:30 P.M. daily.

TASTINGS: Complimentary for 4 wines; $2 for reserve wines (applicable to purchase).

TOURS: 10:30 A.M. and 2 P.M. daily.

THE WINES: Barbera, Cabernet Sauvignon, Chardonnay, Cuvée de la Luna (proprietary red blend), Pinot Blanc, Pinot Noir, Port, Rosata Di Sangiovese, Sangiovese, sparkling wine, Syrah, Zinfandel, old-vine Zinfandel.

SPECIALTIES: Cuvée de la Luna, Pinot Blanc, Port.

WINEMAKER: Steve Rued.

ANNUAL PRODUCTION: 40,000 cases.

OF SPECIAL NOTE: Annual events include Barrel Tasting (March), Festa Italia (July), Harvest Moon (October). Barbera, Port, and sparkling wine available only at winery.

NEARBY ATTRACTIONS: Jack London Historic State Park (museum, hiking, horseback riding); Sonoma Valley Regional Park (hiking, dog park); Mission San Francisco Solano and other historic buildings in downtown Sonoma.

VIANSA WINERY & ITALIAN MARKETPLACE

VIANSA WINERY & ITALIAN MARKETPLACE
25200 Arnold Dr.
Sonoma, CA 95476
800-995-4740
Tuscan@viansa.com
www.viansa.com

OWNER: The 360 Global Co.

LOCATION: 5 miles south of the town of Sonoma.

APPELLATION: Sonoma Valley.

HOURS: 10 A.M.–5 P.M. daily.

TASTINGS: $5 for 4 wines; $10 for 4 reserve wines.

TOURS: 11 A.M. and 2:15 P.M. daily ($5).

THE WINES: Aleatico, Arneis, Barbera, Cabernet Franc, Cabernet Sauvignon, Chardonnay, Dolcetto, Frescolina, Merlot, Nebbiolo, Pinot Grigio, Pinot Noir, Primitivo, Sangiovese, Tocai.

SPECIALTY: Italian varietals.

WINEMAKER: Derek Irwin.

ANNUAL PRODUCTION: 60,000 cases.

OF SPECIAL NOTE: All wines sold exclusively at tasting room. Picnic area; extensive selection of gourmet foods sold in market. Tours of wetlands. Barbecues and live music held Friday through Sunday during summer months.

NEARBY ATTRACTIONS: Mission San Francisco Solano and other historic buildings in downtown Sonoma; Infineon Raceway (NASCAR and other events); biplane flights; Cornerstone Festival of Gardens (high-concept landscape installations).

The Sonoma Valley, with its gentle hills, olive groves, and abundant vineyards, is often compared to Tuscany. Nowhere is that comparison more apt than at Viansa, which could be mistaken for a tiny village in the Italian countryside. Perched atop a knoll at the southern entrance to the valley, the winery's tile-roofed terra-cotta villa was painstakingly modeled after an ancient Tuscan convent. The effect is underscored by extensive plantings of stone pines and Italian cypress trees.

Viansa Winery and Italian Marketplace opened in 1990 and, for the first few years, offered an array of both California and Italian varietals. By increasing its focus on the latter, the winery now produces the largest selection of Italian varietals of any California winery. Wines such as Sangiovese and Pinot Grigio, as well as lesser-known ones like Arneis and Primitivo, are poured at two tasting bars in the Italian Marketplace, along with an array of California varietals, including Chardonnay and Merlot. The marketplace, a grand hall graced with hand-painted murals, massive beams, and Italian marble, is a showplace for Viansa's impressive line of Cal-Ital culinary treats. From pestos and aiolis to salsas, marinades, and dessert sauces, the display underscores the winery's philosophy that wine should be served with good food. Viansa also produces estate-grown oil made from olives harvested from some thousand olive trees on the property. Generous samples of many condiments are available throughout the marketplace.

Focaccia, cheeses, olives, and other snacks can be purchased at the deli counter. For heartier fare, the *cucina* (Italian kitchen) prepares fresh salads, sandwiches, tortas, and desserts such as triple-chocolate cookies. These can be enjoyed with Viansa wines at one of the many picnic tables in the shade of an arbor on the north side of the villa. From this hilltop perch, called Alto Piano, picnickers can appreciate the views of Sonoma Valley.

Directly north of the winery are ninety acres of lowlands that are flooded on a seasonal basis, rendering the site useless for grape growing. In 1992 Viansa began converting the former hay field to the county's largest privately owned, freshwater wetlands. Situated on the Pacific Flyway, the ninety-acre preserve supports a variety of wildlife, including jackrabbits and muskrats as well as owls, egrets, tundra swans, golden eagles, Canada geese, and several species of ducks. In all, more than 150 avian species have been spotted here, with as many as 13,000 birds visiting each day during peak migratory periods in winter and spring. Guided tours of the wetlands are offered from February through May, and participants are encouraged to bring binoculars on the outings.

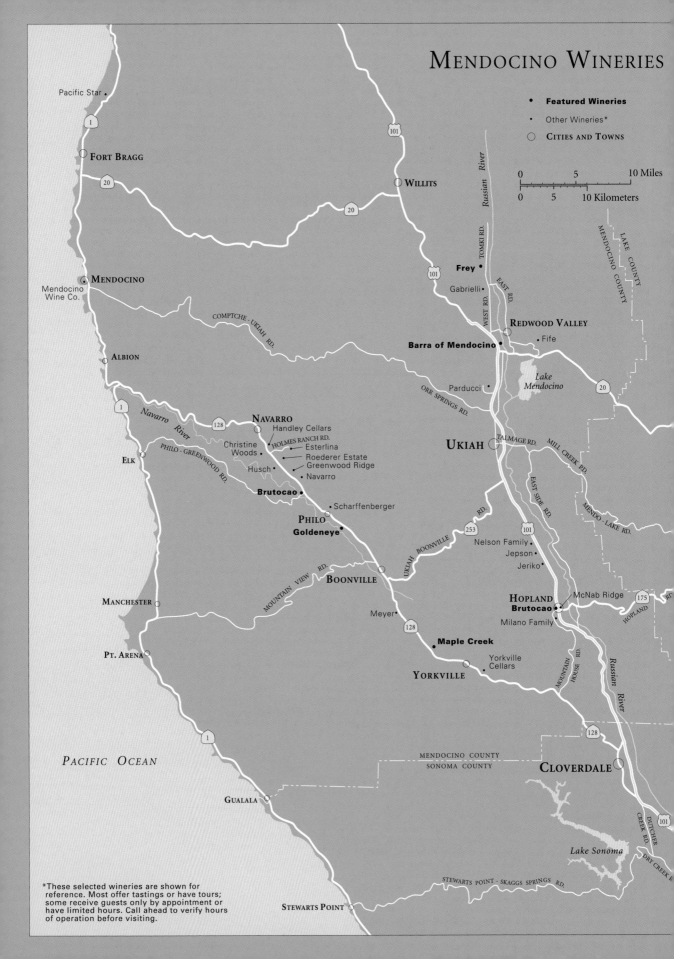

MENDOCINO WINERIES

- ● **Featured Wineries**
- • Other Wineries*
- ○ CITIES AND TOWNS

0   5   10 Miles

0   5   10 Kilometers

Pacific Star •

① 1

FORT BRAGG

② 20

WILLITS

20

Russian River

101

Frey •

Gabrielli •

MENDOCINO

Mendocino Wine Co.

WEST RD.

EAST RD.

TOMKI RD.

REDWOOD VALLEY

Barra of Mendocino •

• Fife

COMPTCHE - UKIAH RD.

ALBION

Lake Mendocino

20

Parducci •

ORR SPRINGS RD.

Navarro River

1

128

NAVARRO

Handley Cellars

HOLMES RANCH RD.

Christine Woods

Esterlina

Roederer Estate

Greenwood Ridge

Husch

Navarro

UKIAH

TALMAGE RD.

MILL CREEK RD.

PHILO - GREENWOOD RD.

ELK

Brutocao •

• Scharffenberger

PHILO

Goldeneye •

EAST SIDE RD.

MENDO - LAKE RD.

RD.

253

101

Nelson Family •

Jepson •

Jeriko •

MANCHESTER

MOUNTAIN VIEW RD.

UKIAH BOONVILLE

BOONVILLE

Meyer •

128

HOPLAND

Brutocao •

McNab Ridge •

175

Milano Family •

HOPLAND

PT. ARENA

Maple Creek •

Yorkville Cellars •

MOUNTAIN HOUSE RD.

Russian River

YORKVILLE

PACIFIC OCEAN

MENDOCINO COUNTY

SONOMA COUNTY

CLOVERDALE

128

101

GUALALA

DUTCHER CREEK RD.

Lake Sonoma

DRY CREEK R.

STEWARTS POINT - SKAGGS SPRINGS RD.

STEWARTS POINT

*These selected wineries are shown for reference. Most offer tastings or have tours; some receive guests only by appointment or have limited hours. Call ahead to verify hours of operation before visiting.

Inland Mendocino has been slower to catch national attention than the county's dramatic coastline, but that is changing as local winemakers are proving their grapes are on a par with those of Sonoma and Napa. There remains something of a pioneer spirit here, a love of the great outdoors that is reflected in a serious respect for the environment. It is no wonder that Mendocino leads the nation in farming organic vineyards.

Mendocino now has nearly forty wineries, many of them located off the beaten path in the shelter of redwoods or beside rivers. Most of the county is an undevel- oped, pristine landscape with abundant oppor- tunities for enjoying an endless variety of outdoor pursuits: hiking, fishing, camping, watersports, or a quiet walk along a secluded beach.

Wine grapes were first planted here in the middle of the nineteenth century, some by immigrants drawn to California by the 1849 Gold Rush. These farmers tended to plant food crops on the flat river plains and to position their vineyards on the more rugged hillsides and sun-exposed ridgetops. In time, they and their successors found fertile ground in the cooler Anderson Valley west of Hopland and Ukiah. The growing conditions vary so greatly between these two regions that Mendocino winemakers have found success with a wide spectrum of grape varietals.

BARRA OF MENDOCINO

BARRA OF MENDOCINO
7051 North State St.
Redwood Valley, CA 95470
707-485-0322
info@barraofmendocino.
com
www.barraofmendocino.
com

OWNERS: Charles and
Martha Barra.

LOCATION: 5 miles north of
Ukiah via Hwy. 101.

APPELLATION:
Redwood Valley.

HOURS: 9:30 A.M.–5:30 P.M.
daily.

TASTINGS: Complimentary.

TOURS: By appointment.

THE WINES: Cabernet
Sauvignon, Chardonnay,
Muscat Canelli, Petite
Sirah, Pinot Blanc, Pinot
Noir, Port, Sangiovese,
Zinfandel.

SPECIALTIES: Petite Sirah,
Pinot Noir.

WINEMAKER: Various
consulting winemakers.

ANNUAL PRODUCTION:
11,000 cases.

OF SPECIAL INTEREST:
Gardens with picnic area.
Gift shop with wine accessories, gourmet food, and
apparel. Annual events
include A Taste of Red-
wood Valley (June, on
Father's Day weekend);
Sunset at the Cellars (July);
and wild mushroom
gourmet dinners with
guest chefs (November).

NEARBY ATTRACTIONS:
Real Goods Solar Living
Center (tours, store);
Lake Mendocino (hiking,
boating, fishing, camping);
Grace Hudson Museum
(Pomo Indian baskets,
historical photographs,
changing art exhibits);
Vichy Springs (mineral
springs and resort).

Few, if any, people in the wine business can challenge Charlie Barra's record: he's been growing grapes since 1945. That's what gave him and his wife, Martha, the idea for a brand-new wine, "59th Harvest." Using grapes from the 2004 harvest, it is a highly stylized Pinot Noir with bold, concentrated flavors, in contrast to the more subtle profile of Burgundian Pinots. Plans call for the label to change every year; the 2005 vintage will get its own label, "60th Harvest," and so on.

Even after all these years, the Barras find new things to do with the grapes they grow organically on their 175-acre home ranch,  Redwood Valley Vineyards. They are also coming out with another new brand, Girasole Vineyards. That concept was born of the Pinot Noir glut of 2001 that forced many growers to make a difficult choice: bottle the wine or sell it at drastically reduced prices. The Barras decided to use their Pinot Noir to make a less expensive wine, one with fresh, bright flavors and its own name, which means "sunflower" in Italian. The Barras are also introducing a vintage port, starting with the 2005 Petite Sirah, which they intend to release by 2007.

The wine world has changed dramatically since Charlie Barra picked up his first pair of pruning shears. Barra was born almost eighty years ago to Italian immigrant parents who were accustomed to hard work in the vineyards. They were attracted to the area because of its resemblance to Italy's Piedmont region. As they farmed their new land, they were rewarded with a climate whose warm days and cool nights allow the grapes to mature at a slow pace, thus producing intense flavors.

Barra, like many other Mendocino grape growers, came to embrace a steward-of-the-land view of farming, a down-to-earth attitude that propelled him toward sustainable agriculture. Aware that chemical pesticides were endangering the long-term vitality of his land, Barra stopped using them in 1985. Redwood Valley Vineyards is certified annually by the California Certified Organic Farmers (CCOF).

Barra of Mendocino, which has grown from two hundred cases a year to eleven thousand, opened its tasting room in 1995 two miles down the road from Redwood Valley Vineyards. The structure was built in 1972 by Weibel Champagne Cellars, which may explain why it looks like an inverted shallow Champagne glass (minus the long stem). Beneath the circular roof is a five-thousand-square-foot room with massive beams sweeping toward the ceiling and a fountain in the center. Outside, an expansive lawn and a carefully tended garden surround picnic tables that can seat up to 180 people.

BRUTOCAO CELLARS

BRUTOCAO CELLARS
13500 Hwy. 101
Hopland, CA 95449
800-433-3689
7000 Hwy. 128
Philo, CA 95466
707-895-2152
brutocao@pacific.net
www.brutocaocellars.com

OWNER: Leonard Brutocao.

LOCATION: U.S. 101 in downtown Hopland; Hwy. 128 in Anderson Valley.

APPELLATION: Mendocino.

HOURS: 10 A.M.–5 P.M. daily.

TASTINGS: Complimentary.

TOURS: By appointment.

THE WINES: Cabernet Sauvignon, Chardonnay, Merlot, Pinot Noir, Port, Primitivo, Sauvignon Blanc, Syrah, Zinfandel.

SPECIALTIES: Cabernet Sauvignon, Merlot, Zinfandel.

WINEMAKER: Fred Nickel.

ANNUAL PRODUCTION: 12,000 cases.

OF SPECIAL NOTE: Crushed Grape Restaurant serving wood-fired pizza and California cuisine. Annual events include Valentine's Day Crabfeed (February), Hopland Passport (May and October), Anderson Valley Pinot Noir Festival (May), Big Bottles and Bocce BBQ (June), School Benefit Bocce Tourney (September), Port and Chocolate Tasting (November). Port and Syrah available only at tasting rooms.

NEARBY ATTRACTIONS: Real Goods Solar Living Center (tours, store); Hendy Woods State Park (redwood groves, hiking, camping).

Downtown Hopland was a quiet place with only a hotel, two modest restaurants, a brew pub, and the odd antique shop until the Brutocao family came to town. The Brutocaos, who had been making wine under their own label and already operated a tasting room in nearby Anderson Valley, decided to establish a presence on U.S. 101.

In 1997 Brutocao Cellars purchased the old Hopland High School from the Fetzer wine family and began creating a seven-and-a-half-acre complex dedicated to food and wine. Schoolhouse Plaza opened two years later with a tasting room, a gift shop, and the Crushed Grape Restaurant in the remodeled 1920s building, which still has its original facade bearing the high school's name. On display in the tasting room and restaurant are memorabilia from the school's glory days. The complex also includes a coffee shop, an art gallery, and a store featuring locally made prod- ucts. Visitors can sip coffee while perusing the racks in the adjacent visitors' center.

The Brutocaos, who trace their heritage to Italy, brought more than a love of food and wine when they came to this country. They are also passionate about bocce ball, a devilishly challenging game with a half-century Italian lineage. The com- plex has six regulation bocce (pro- nounced (BOTCH-ee) courts, which are lighted and open to the public.

With the remodeling complete, the winery set to work landscaping the grounds with some six thousand lavender plants and thirty-four hundred rosebushes. Between the terraces and the bocce ball courts is an expanse of manicured lawn with a peaked-roof gazebo that is used for weddings and other special events.

Brutocao Cellars is a tale of two families who combined their skills and expertise to establish one of Mendocino County's most notable wineries. The Brutocaos immigrated from Venice in the early 1900s, bringing with them a passion for wine. Len Brutocao met Marty Bliss while in school at Berkeley. Marty's father, Irv, had been farming land in Mendocino since the 1940s. Len and Marty married, and soon thereafter the families joined forces and began to grow grapes. The family sold their grapes to other wineries for years before starting to make their own wine in 1991. They selected the Lion of St. Mark from St. Mark's Cathedral in Venice as their symbol of family tradition and quality. The heart of that quality, they say, is in their 575 acres of vineyards in southern Mendocino County and another 12 acres (of Pinot Noir) in Anderson Valley. The original tasting room in Philo is still in use. With its high-beamed ceilings and wisteria-covered patio, it makes an ideal stop for those traveling scenic Highway 128 to the Pacific Coast.

FREY VINEYARDS, LTD.

FREY VINEYARDS, LTD.
14000 Tomki Rd.
Redwood Valley, CA 95470
707-485-5177
800-760-3739
info@freywine.com
www.freywine.com

OWNERS: Frey family.

LOCATION: 14 miles north of Ukiah off U.S. 101.

APPELLATION:
Redwood Valley.

HOURS: By appointment.

TASTINGS: Complimentary.

TOURS: By appointment.

THE WINES: Cabernet Sauvignon, Chardonnay, Gewürztraminer, Merlot, Petite Sirah, Pinot Noir, Sangiovese, Sauvignon Blanc, Syrah, Zinfandel.

SPECIALTIES: Certified organic wines without added sulfites; biodynamically grown estate-bottled wines.

WINEMAKERS: Paul and Jonathan Frey.

ANNUAL PRODUCTION: 60,000 cases.

OF SPECIAL NOTE: Picnic area for visitors' use; biodynamic aromatherapy products made from vineyard-grown herbs sold at winery.

NEARBY ATTRACTIONS: Real Goods Solar Living Center (tours, store); Lake Mendocino (hiking, boating, fishing, camping); Grace Hudson Museum (Pomo Indian baskets, historical photographs, changing art exhibits); Vichy Springs (mineral springs and resort); Orr Hot Springs (mineral springs spa).

Arguably the most low-key winery in California, this gem is hidden off a two-lane road that wends through an undeveloped corner of Redwood Valley. Unsuspecting visitors might mistake the first building for the tasting room, but that's grandma's house. They must drive past it to reach the winery, and upon arriving, they find that there is no formal tasting room. Instead, tastings are conducted outdoors at a couple of planks set over a pair of wine barrels. When temperatures drop or rain falls, everyone retires to the original house—a redwood structure fashioned from an old barn—where the senior Mrs. Frey lives. Visitors are encouraged to picnic at one of several redwood tables and benches hand-hewn by the late family patriarch, Paul.

Virtually everything at this winery seems handmade or fashioned from something else. Barrels and tanks have been salvaged from larger operations, and the winery itself was constructed of redwood from a defunct winery in Ukiah. Some rows of grapevines are interplanted with herbs such as sage and oregano, which are harvested and distilled into aromatherapy products.

Frey (pronounced "fry") Vineyards is the oldest and largest all-organic winery in the United States. It may have another claim to fame as the winery with the most family members on the payroll. In 1961, Paul and Marguerite Frey, both doctors, bought ninety-nine acres near the headwaters of the Russian River. The Redwood Valley property seemed a great place to raise a family. Five of the couple's twelve children were born after the move, and most are still in the neighborhood.

In 1965 the Freys planted forty acres of Cabernet Sauvignon and Grey Riesling grapevines on the ranch's old pastureland, but they didn't start making wine until the 1970s. Eldest son Jonathan, who studied organic viticulture, began tending the vineyards and harvesting the grapes, which at first were sold to other wineries. When a Cabernet Sauvignon made with their grapes won a gold medal for a Santa Cruz winery, the family realized the vineyard's potential. Frey Vineyards was founded the next year, in 1980.

In 1996 the family began farming biodynamically. The word *biodynamic* stems from the agricultural theories of Austrian scientist and educator Rudolf Steiner. Biodynamic practices undertake to restore vitality to the soil. The farm is managed as a self-sustaining ecosystem, using special composting methods and specific planting times. As good stewards of the land, Frey started the first organic winery and was the first American winery fully certified by Demeter, the biodynamic certification organization. The wines have won many gold and silver medals for excellence.

GOLDENEYE WINERY

In a rural valley known for its grazing sheep and oak-dotted hillsides, it's easy to get distracted by the scenery along Highway 128. Drivers heading to the Goldeneye Winery, however, have only to watch for one landmark: a long, white fence that looks as if it belongs on a thoroughbred horse ranch in Kentucky bluegrass country.

Situated adjacent to the headwaters of the Navarro River, formed on the western edge of the property where Ander-son Creek and Rancheria Creek flow together, the eighty-acre Confluence pitality center is in the orig-that dates to the 1930s. True the style of the interior is period-style furnishings, in-style lampshades. Glossy

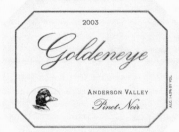

property is home to the Vineyard. Goldeneye's hos-inal single-story farmhouse to the structure's vintage, updated craftsman, with cluding distinctive Tiffany-hardwood floors extend to windows that overlook the vineyards. The walls are hung with paintings of valley scenes and the winery's namesake goldeneye ducks.

The nomenclature is not surprising, considering that Goldeneye is a sister winery to the Duck-horn Wine Company. In 1990, after making world-class Bordeaux-style wines in the Napa Valley for fifteen years, Dan and Margaret Duckhorn decided to indulge their growing passion for Pinot Noir. Their goal was to craft a uniquely California Pinot equal in stature to their acclaimed Duckhorn Vineyards Merlot. The Duckhorns, aware that Pinot Noir tends to reflect its *terroir* (the place where it is grown) more than most wines, spent the next six years experimenting with grapes grown in several other appellations. The Anderson Valley's clay soil, cool ocean fog, and long, mild growing season convinced them to plant six acres of grapevines at Confluence in 1996.

In all, the winery farms 150 acres of estate vineyards spread among four ranches in the Ander-son Valley. The best grapes from each are blended into every vintage of Goldeneye Pinot Noir. In 2001 the winery created a sister label, Migration, a Pinot Noir that is crafted as a lighter alternative to the rich, structured Goldeneye. Current vintages of both wines are served at a long table in the comfortable tasting room, along with complementary seasonal foods.

Guests are welcome to stroll outside and picnic on the landscaped terrace, or simply enjoy the view of the vineyards and picturesque old apple-drying barn from one of the Adirondack chairs that suggest the relaxed pace of this secluded region. Even now, Anderson Valley is rarely, if ever, crowded, making it a prime destination for wine lovers seeking personal attention and a leisurely visit.

GOLDENEYE WINERY
9200 Highway 128
Philo, CA 95466
707-895-3202
800-208-0438
hospitality@goldeneye
winery.com
www.goldeneyewinery.
com

OWNER: Duckhorn
Wine Company.

LOCATION: 5 miles north-west of Boonville.

APPELLATION:
Anderson Valley.

HOURS: 11 A.M.–4 P.M. daily.

TASTINGS: $5.

TOURS: None.

THE WINE: Pinot Noir.

SPECIALTY: Pinot Noir.

WINEMAKER:
Zach Rasmuson.

ANNUAL PRODUCTION:
10,000 cases.

OF SPECIAL NOTE: Picnic
area. Sampling of artisanal
food with wine tasting.
Migration Vin Gris of
Pinot Noir available only
at winery. Annual events
include Pinot Noir
Festival (May).

NEARBY ATTRACTIONS:
Hendy Woods State
Park (hiking, swimming,
camping).

MAPLE CREEK WINERY

MAPLE CREEK WINERY
20799 Hwy. 128
Yorkville CA 95494
707-895-3001
Linda@maplecreekwine.
com; Tom@maplecreek
wine.com
www.artevinowine.com
www.maplecreekwine.com

OWNERS: Tom Rodrigues
and Linda Stutz.

LOCATION: 22 miles west of
Cloverdale via Hwy. 128.

APPELLATION:
Yorkville Highlands.

HOURS: 10:30 A.M.–5 P.M.
daily; shorter hours in the
winter months.

TASTINGS: $3 (applicable
to purchase).

TOURS: None.

THE WINES: Chardonnay,
Merlot, Pinot Noir, Sym-
phony (hybrid of Muscat
and Grenache Gris),
Zinfandel.

SPECIALTIES: Estate Chardonnay, late-harvest wines,
Bordeaux-style reds.

WINEMAKERS:
Tom Rodrigues; Kerry
Damskey, consulting
winemaker.

ANNUAL PRODUCTION:
3,500 cases.

OF SPECIAL NOTE: Art
gallery featuring works by
owner/winemaker Tom
Rodrigues. Picnic tables.
Most of the wines available
only at the tasting room.
Local events include Crab
and Wine Days (January),
Yorkville Highlands Wine
Festival (August), and
Mushroom and Wine Days
(November).

NEARBY ATTRACTIONS:
Hendy Woods State Park
(redwood groves, hiking,
camping).

In late winter and early spring, drivers along scenic Highway 128 can see young lambs cavorting in the fields, a sure sign of impending warm weather. Throughout the year, apple and pear orchards, small farms, and winding roads make this part of Mendocino one of the most beautiful drives in California. It is characterized by small, family-owned wineries where the owners and winemakers are often available to meet visitors. Life at Maple Creek is so casual, in fact, that if you arrive in the winter months, you may be greeted by a sign that reads "Honk For Wine."

That potential for an intimate experience was one of the factors in Linda Stutz's and Tom Rodrigues's decision to open their own winery. The couple met at a party in 1995, when both were pursuing their own careers. Stutz was  designing commercial interiors in San Francisco. Rodrigues had established himself as a successful artist in media ranging from stained glass to wine labels, such as those for Far Niente and its sister winery, Nickel & Nickel, in Napa Valley.

By 2001 Stutz and Rodrigues were ready for a radical change. When the old Martz family property came on the market, they recognized a good business opportunity. The 180-acre parcel included seven natural springs and was far from the hectic urban environment of the San Francisco Bay Area. Today, they own 12 acres of vineyards that produce fruit for the winery's award-winning Merlot, Zinfandel, and Chardonnay.

Stutz and Rodrigues named their winery after the creek that runs year-round through their hilly property and set to work transforming an old farm building into a rustic tasting room. They decorated it with numerous paintings and other works by Rodrigues, ranging from a portrait of baseball player Cool Papa Bell (the original hangs in the Hall of Fame in Cooperstown, New York) to pastoral scenes of Anderson Valley, which adorn the winery's Artevino label. Rodrigues and Stutz chose the name to represent their twin interests.

Rodrigues was introduced to wine as a youngster. His grandparents earned their living growing fruit, and wine was regarded as merely one more food product on the dining room table. By the time he was an adult, Rodrigues had become a serious wine consumer and collector. He is still learning, thanks to his winemaking consultant, Kerry Damskey, who has done similar work for prestigious labels such as Flora Springs and Preston.

Rodrigues and Stutz, like a handful of colleagues in the sparsely populated Yorkville Highlands appellation, have become not only vintners but ranchers and art dealers as well. That their nearest neighbors are at least a mile away suits them just fine.

ACKNOWLEDGMENTS

Creativity, perseverance, and commitment are important qualities for
guaranteeing the success of a project. The artistic and editorial team who worked on this edition
possess these qualities in large measures. My heartfelt thanks go to Marty Olmstead, writer;
Robert Holmes, photographer; Jennifer Beales, designer; Judith Dunham, copy editor;
Carrie Bradley, proofreader; and Ben Pease, cartographer.

In addition, I am grateful for the invaluable counsel of Greg Taylor; William Silberkleit;
Estelle Silberkleit; my late-night crisis administrator, Danny Biederman; and the scores of readers and
winery enthusiasts who have contacted me to say how much they enjoy this book series.

And finally, for their love, support, and creative input, as well as for enduring work-filled weekends
and midnight deadlines, my gratitude and affection go to Gent and Lisa Silberkleit.

—Tom Silberkleit

Photographs copyright © 2006 by Robert Holmes
Text and maps copyright © 2006 by Wine House Press
All rights reserved. No text, photographs, maps, or other
portions of this book may be reproduced in any form
without the written permission of the publisher.

Wine House Press
127 East Napa Street, Suite F, Sonoma, CA 95476
707-996-1741

Editor and publisher: Tom Silberkleit
Original design: Jennifer Barry Design, Fairfax, CA
Design and production: Jennifer Beales
Copy editor: Judith Dunham
Maps: Ben Pease
Proofreader: Carrie Bradley

All photographs by Robert Holmes except the following:
page 16: creativedirections.com; page 27, bottom left:
Marvin Collins; page 31, bottom left: Lenny Siegel
Photographic; page 32, bottom left: Rick Bolen; page 40,
bottom right: Adrian Gregorutti; page 52, bottom left:
Rick Bolen; pages 54 and 55: ©John Sutton 2006; page
60, bottom left, and page 61: Robert Mondavi Winery;
page 64, bottom right: Brian Bosen; page 68, bottom
right: Caitlin McCaffrey; pages 74 and 75: creativedirec-
tions.com; page 88, bottom left: Bill Dungan; page 92,
bottom right: Chris Vomvolakis; page 99, bottom left:
Stacey Chapin; page 104, bottom right: Chris Vomvolakis;
pages 114 and 115: M. J. Wickham; page 124, bottom
right: Pradoe Advertising and Design; pages 140 and 141:
Belinda Weber.

Front cover photograph: Vineyards in Los Carneros, Napa
Back cover photographs: top left: Nickel & Nickel;
top right: Spring Mountain; bottom left: Spring Mountain;
bottom right: Mumm Napa.

Printed and bound in Singapore through DNP America,
LLC

ISBN-10: 0-9724993-3-4
ISBN-13: 978-0-9724993-3-0

Third Edition

Distributed by Ten Speed Press, P.O. Box 7123, Berkeley, CA
94707, www.tenspeed.com

The publisher has made every effort to ensure the accuracy
of the information contained in *The California Directory of
Fine Wineries,* but can accept no liability for any loss, injury,
or inconvenience sustained by any visitor as a result of any
information or recommendation contained in this guide.
Travelers should always call ahead to confirm hours of operation, fees, and other highly variable information.

Always act responsibly when drinking alcoholic beverages by
selecting a designated driver or prearranged transportation.

Customized Editions
Wine House Press will print custom editions of this volume
for bulk purchase at your request. Personalized covers and
foil-stamped corporate logo imprints can be created in large
quantities for special promotions or events, or as premiums.
For more information, contact Custom Imprints, Wine
House Press, 127 E. Napa Street, Suite F, Sonoma, CA 95476;
707-996-1741.